MW01536226

The Mysterious Murder of Marilyn Monroe

.

by Ana C. Antunes

This is a work of fiction based upon facts. Any names, places and events are NOT merely coincidental and the story told can actually be quite true while the actual History made by hoax and deceptions still proves to keep deceits treated as reality.

Title: "The Mysterious Murder of Marilyn Monroe"
Author: Ana Claudia Antunes
Copyright © 2011 Ana Claudia Antunes
All rights reserved.

ISBN: 978-1-329-05119-5

Dance As One
http://dance-as-one.blogspot.com

Author 's profile:
https://www.goodreads.com/AnaAntunes

Amazon's Author Page:
http://www.amazon.com/Ana-Claudia-Antunes/e/B002DBHE30

Ana´s Books
http://www.lulu.com/spotlight/virtualbookstore

It's time to put some light on a very dark issue which has the collective unconscious in a blast for quite a while now. This novel is based upon the Conspiracy Theories which involve the mysterious assassination of JFK, the September Eleven Tragedy up to the Sniper Case in Washington D.C. and beyond.

Novel, Screenplay and film by Ana C.

In the year 1962, the year of the Tiger by the Chinese Horoscope, right in the middle of the cold war, a violent World Cup took place in Chile, and it was also a scenario of a strange crime.

Before Brazil won the World Championship for the second time, Pele, already famous as the best soccer player of all times, got injured in the second game against Czechoslovak. Meanwhile, a high member of the Czechoslovakian football team was found dead in his hotel room in Valparaiso. He was forty-four years old. He was tall, elegant, a traveler as a government worker, with a close relationship with the Dalai Lama.
A sculpture with a secret message that was left in the hotel's safety for the Ambassador of Chile in India was gone. It was a statue of an enlightened divine being with a somewhat alien appearance, representing Siddha, the most elevated form of being, surpassing all mundane matters, the highest point possible. It was also the symbol of a secret order believed to have existed, and still active, with members remaining somewhere in the Himalayan mountains of Tibet.
The main suspected, a Chilean woman who became Czechoslovakian citizen for more than twenty years, and who supposedly worked for the Communist cause and kept private matters between the Russians until she met her deceased husband. Once in love with him, she decided to devote her life for him instead.
Soon after China ceased fire in the Sino-Indian Border Conflict War, the mysterious woman disappeared. Would she also be involved in the conflict or was she working as a spy the whole time? Was she a member of the black order which was not only related to Marilyn Monroe mysterious murder but also to what became the most undercover case of conspiracy from all times history, the assassination of JFK?

"I'm selfish, impatient and a little insecure. I make mistakes, I am out of control and at times hard to handle. But if you can't handle me at my worst, then you sure as hell don't deserve me at my best."
—Marilyn Monroe

1

When you wish upon a Star

Juno, the first Goddess of the Pantheon, thought it was a good idea to come down to Earth. So she decided to take the form of a human being, the most enchanting one, just to compete with her counterpart Venus. It was then that on a hot day, the first of June 1926, in the year of the Fire Tiger, a baby named Norma Jeane was born in Los Angeles, California.

Thirty-six years later, more three times the year of the Tiger would pass by, and in the same city of the Angels, after becoming a sex-symbol and a bombshell, then internationally famous and acclaimed movie star, Marilyn Monroe dies in the same year of the Tiger, only it was ruled by the water tiger, somewhat an iconic irony having water putting out the fire. And she was blown off like a candle in the middle of a hurricane.

After all, she knew too much and she was already pulling the buttons of anymore and any less than the most important figure in the world history, the President of the United States. And she kept all her/(and his) secrets on the diary, the same one he did spell during their love-making and that she wrote the annotations in a small red book, as her doctor himself told her to do.

1

It´s then when she decided to reveal it all to the press, after many rejections and humiliations from both the president and his brother, Bob Kennedy. In the middle of the night, when she had just announced to a close friend, to whom she had been talking on her only true friend, her phone, she received an unexpected visit from both her doctor and the Senator, who was accompanied by his brother-in-law. This one she knew too well, an actor whose participation in her life included the many ventures and adventures of a self-proclaimed "Rat Pack".

The weekend previous to her assassination, she was invited to spend at a friend's house in Lake Tahoe. It was anyone else but Frank Sinatra, the mastermind of all things related to the Rat Pack. When he invited her, he had already introduced her to the Mob. And he had planned to make it an incidental encounter between her and Sam Giancana, after taking his private jet to Cal-Neva Lodge.

Giancana talked to her in private and told her about the perils of overexposing herself the way she did in May when she sang the most gossiped event of the year, a "Happy Birthday, Mr. President" in her utmost ironical futility tempered by her hyper-sexually charged tone. Of course, the idea was to provoke. At least, that's what Peter, the president's brother-in-law and also member of the Rat Pack, had in mind. But what he didn't expect it was the reaction from Marilyn when she insinuated herself towards the issue, with the entire crowd in an ovation during the Birthday of the President, with her dress sculpted in her voluptuous body, upsetting him to the bones. That's when he have decided that she was getting way too close to his own business and it was time to call it quits. He left the matter to his brother's hands, since his brother-in-law, Peter, was too scared of her other friends and way too involved with the diva to be left on taking care of her moves. Apparently Frank was the first to try to warn her about the dangers if she continued to behave the way she did towards the Kennedy's.

"Yes, I remember every word that he told me like it was yesterday. "Listen, baby", he said, "I would hate to see you in trouble. Why don't you just stop now? I don't see what the point of you being involved into Politics is." You don´t see what is the point? I should have shouted out and laughed at his face.

And then I told him. "Mind your own business. It's not about Politics, it's about Love." I know he's in love with me. He told me so. He didn't say that he would leave his wife or the Congress for me, but hey, I didn't expect anything else from him. It is not that we had planned to get married or stuff. Besides, he's way too shy to even try to give the first step. We did make love once, and he left me, he didn't want to answer my calls. I'm just-- -it's just that I couldn't talk to him. I so want to talk to him about so many things. He wouldn't listen to me. I guess that it isn't fair for me.

Now I got all this information inside my mind and I cannot stop thinking about this, that I've got a mission here. I just have to get all this information out there. People deserve to know. I always believed I belonged to the world, to my public. The stuff, the secrets I know, they cannot be kept private for too long. I must tell— I ought to tell everyone about this. It's burning me inside. And I've got to get this out of my system one way or another.

Frank was trying to protect me. I know it. But I was too stubborn at that time; I knew it was hard to help me like that bit I know he tried to persuade me to shut up. So he took me to Sam. It was his last shot. And he was all kind to me at first. But as I didn't agree with him he simply told me, "Do whatever you have to do. I'm cleaning my case here and washing my hands. I would hate to see you suffering, and I would try to avoid you getting hurt in any way possible. But if you insist on telling people about this story, I cannot do anything but leave." And he left that very evening. It was the last time I saw him. It would be the last time I would see anyone. If I could have only listened to what he had to tell me… I was really too stubborn. At least I wouldn't be dead by now... that's for sure. Besides, I would rather live until I could feel safe enough to reveal the secrets that I was so eagerly waiting to burst out than to be shutdown and out of the way just like they did to me. But I guess that was also part of the plan. I'm a firm believer things happen the way they do for a purpose. If what happened to me would have any significance it was to show to those who thought that making me shut up would stop people from loving me, they were completely wrong. It was then that my fans and admirers really showed all their support to the woman I was. And that for me was worth the whole show. Don't be sad, I'm glad I had lived a life where I was a victim and a *femme fatale* at the same time, just like the anti-heroines that I've been portraying in the movies. I wouldn't expect anything less than this. And that would include a tragic end? Why not! This part I wish I could erase, but I guess they all have a significant role for the collective consciousness. The public needed that to reaffirm what's like to be victimized by society. I know for sure that it was all written before I was even born Norma Jeane."

On July 7th, 1962 a photographer arrives at her Brentwood home for what turned out to be her very last photo session, a shooting in her own house which was made for a LIFE cover. Marilyn was on the telephone, as she usually was, chatting with her VIP friends and colleagues. Eunice Murray, her live-in housekeeper and companion, was there then and when Marilyn died. At that fatal moment she was nude but for the photo shooting she wore, as the photographer later revealed in the film, "a tight fitting Capri pants and a dark V-neck sweater." She was fragile and thin, and somewhat succumbed to the Hollywood standards of what a sex-symbol should look like. She looked sad. The interview was scheduled to be published on August 3rd. None would expect she would die two days later... or would they have known just to sell more copies of LIFE! Such irony... As if she would be there, anyway.

And she would die in her house that she had just recently bought, a place that she thought she could finally call a home. A simple, not fancy place, with a private space away from all the glamorous life that was devouring her alive, and when she was still alive she still dreamed that she would live a happy peaceful life.

The house had a Spanish style, built in the nineteen twenty, for a twenty-century family who grew too large and the family with children decided to leave, they were the first to live there, and they had to move. But it was perfect for her, and her dreams of having children, if not from her own, she would adopt one, and they will live happily ever after in that house in Brentwood.

"Yes, I didn't like fancy cars, fancy clothes, super special events, or artificial stuff. I didn't look for a big mansion in Beverly Hills, a house at the beach in Malibu, but a nice one, away from the eyes of the paparazzi. And although my house in the end was all bugged by the secret service and I couldn´t stay away from the big brother with twenty-four hour surveillance over my back, I wanted a small house for me to invite my friends in and make private parties or to just chill out and enjoy their company."

But what she didn't know it was to choose her companions with caution. No one ever told her or helped her to look after herself. And she was alone, not lonely, only alone.

A star... yet alone.

*

Just like a former lover of hers, a billionaire who also died alone, penniless and with no remorse of having had the time of his life, drinking, spending all his family fortune and sleeping with all the most glamorous women of this planet, and still at age 88 he remembers and dwells not on his pitfall but take great pride on his glorious past which includes a rubbed shoulders with Howard Hughes, Ali Khan and Nelson Rockefeller, and other more intimate parts with the likes of Monroe, Mansfield, Rita Hayworth, Ava Gardner and Lana Turner.

When, in 1962, he flew to California to meet his former flame Marilyn Monroe and to escort her to the Venice Film Festival, he had in his luggage a topaz necklace that a jeweler friend had asked him to give her. But upon his landing there, on his triumphal arrival in Los Angeles, Guinle was shocked to learn from the papers of the actress's death.

Having checked in to his usual room at the Beverly Hills Hotel, Guinle recovered his poise; he scanned his address book and telephoned the recently divorced Jayne Mansfield. When they met, he gave her the necklace intended for Marilyn Monroe. Guinle remembered it very well.

"She was delighted", he would say. "We spent the next two years together."

That was the time the US government was worried about the Nazis taken over South America, so they decided that creating the illusion that only Hollywood could build in a few months they could sustain the idea of an America from North to South. But what they didn't expect it was that turning Brazil into a Banana Republic image with a cliché that says, "Yes, we have bananas... bananas for giving and not forgiving, and for selling and not excelling!"

And that would only piss off their allies in the South, at least the intellectual class.

Right when Lee Schubert, the Broadway producer and founder of the Schubert Theater, where Arthur Miller showed up with MM, appeared into the scene. And Sonia Henie was already making millions and her producers pocketing up another billion bucks, and Marilyn Monroe was still not even dreaming of becoming so famous.

Schubert saw the talent and then he took Carmen Miranda to make movies, after the figure-skater Sonia Henie, who was in fact my great-grandmother's cousin or, more specifically my grandfather's mother Louise Henie's cousin (and that will make her what? My fourth cousin?), had seen her presentation at the Casino of Urca in Rio, and they went together to contact her. Only that he would pay only for two of the boys in the band called *Bando da Lua*, which translated would be something like Moon Troupe, and who played for Carmen. She would feel scared and lost if they were not there to play the right tune for her to sing along.

Finally Schubert conceded to Carmen's demand to bring along her own back-up band, the legendary *Bando da Lua* (like a Band of the Moon). At that time there were truly no musicians in the United States capable of rhythmically supporting or harmonizing Brazilian music with any stylistic integrity. *Bando da Lua* was the bedrock of her performances in the United States.

Later on in 1954 in an interview for a Brazilian magazine called "O Mundo Ilustrado" or "The Illustrated World".

"Feeling that the original clothing and beauty of Brazilian music would turn into a huge hit in the U.S., Sonja Henie - the godmother of my success - strenuously insisted with Schubert to

7

hire me." Carmen confessed.

"He did not, but perseverance eventually won by my friend and one day to another I found myself in an American stage, surrounded by applause from all sides. The curious thing is that I feared that putting a *Bahiana* fit would be a tremendous turn off. I even asked a reporter to explain why I put a fantasy so vulgar."

A fabricated image to manipulate the masses. That Carmen Miranda died of depression a year later and that Marilyn Monroe died on the same day almost ten years later doesn't seem a total coincidence.

They were both fabricated bombshells who collapsed in a system, victims of a bigger enterprise, the business machine where the big people make fortunes out of their miseries, not of a miserable life but of a miserable self.

So they were in need of a strategic coup. And for someone to take hold of all the public relations, with the heat and to hit the society not for its glamour or intellect but for its money. And in a time of depression when money was all that mattered, no one better than the richest man in Brazil to solve their puzzle on how to deal with a big nation and control a mentality with all the diversities that it involved.

At the Copacabana Palace, the fabulous hotel in Rio de Janeiro built and founded by Castro Silva and by Octavio Guinle, a luxurious hotel in front of the Copacabana Beach and that had so many rich and famous people, all celebrities from around the world passing through its doors until these days, from Orson Welles to Diana, Princess of Wales, Jorge Guinle, the founder´s nephew, still had the energy to be a gentleman, playing the charming, rich and handsome man he was while conquering so many figures from Hollywood.

WHEN YOU WISH UPON A STAR

There where he made his home and in one of the hotel room there which became his deathbed, he gave an interview to "Daily Telegraph" telling about the fairytale that began in 1942 when Roosevelt asked Nelson Rockefeller to win Latin American support for the war against Hitler. Guinle served as Rockefeller's representative in Brazil and began traveling more frequently to the U.S., where Rockefeller introduced him to powerful studio bosses such as Jack Warner, Louis B. Mayer and Darryl Zanuck. And the rest is history.

Jorge Guinle was born on February 5 1916. His family became immensely rich and had a huge fortune after gaining a 90-year concession to build and operate the port of Santos.

So it was then that they built the Copacabana Palace Hotel in Rio, and a huge mansion at Botafogo, where Jorge grew up. When Franklin Delano Roosevelt visited Brazil in the 1930s, he stayed with the Guinles.

As a young man, Jorge Guinle never worked. Then in 1942, when the American government was concerned to counter Nazi influence in Brazil and Latin America, Nelson Rockefeller persuaded him to work for the Allied cause, at home and in the United States.

Rockefeller and Disney were fellows and also known for their vicious ambitious and worship for money and for trying to maintaining mass propaganda and on controlling the masses with their persuasive ingenious ties.

Although Disney tried in vain to create a friendly character, more specifically and pejoratively speaking (no pun intended here) a parrot displaying Joseph Carioca (*carioca* meaning a person who is from Rio) or Ze Carioca, as it's known in Brazil, dancing among *tucanos,* some black birds with enormous yellow plastic-like beaks and beautiful round blue eyes, not even that helped to connect people with America.

THE MYSTERIOUS MURDER OF MM

By the chords of an *Aquarela do Brasil* and also having Sonia
Henie figure skating spectacular dancing in her shows like
Carmen Miranda proved to be big flaws to the foreign
diplomacy. That good neighbor policy was a fluke in the ocean
of despair around the WWII.

No wonder Disney created Ze Carioca in the Copacabana Palace.
He has been secretly working with the elite in Brazil to acting
against M&M... no cookies or chocolates here and not even
Marilyn Monroe, but Marx and Mao, as Communism seemed to
have already had been infiltrated deep in the roots of South
America.

So for this matter, Guinle had to (such a big effort) work, and he
was obliged to go travel between Los Angeles and Rio de
Janeiro. Rio at that time didn't have the slums that are so famous
now, and it was one of the most splendorous, full of life,
ebullient, charming, glamorous and exciting cities in the world.

And Hollywood, yet charming and glamorous but not as
exciting, still with plenty of brightness coming from the
scintillated dressed from the divas.

Those were two cities with plentiful potentially extravaganza for
a man with that amount of money and charm.

And surely his wealth and polished manners would turn heads
towards him, and leave him living the American dream, of
course his paying his fortune and burning his money had a big
deal to do with that too. But who is judging? It´s no secret that if
you are rich and famous people will surround you with goodies.

And he had it all. From gorgeous women to free access to
private clubs and restaurants. And he was one of many; even
Dean Martin had this kind of privilege. Even with no money he
would be invited to have dinner in a fancy restaurant just
because of who he was.

Only telling the truth as crude and gruesome and sometimes
filled with fake stars, with no brilliance at all.

WHEN YOU WISH UPON A STAR

They were actually not as bright as a real star, with the likes of Marilyn Monroe, who was as rich and awesome from the inside as she was seeing from the outside world, with her inner beauty been reflected upon the spotlight from the external ambiance.

And the studios were no different. They spotted a chance in Guinle´s meritorious fortune as well. So they soon gave his empty hands (or full hands, filled with dollar bills) a chance to do something productive, and he started working for the first time in his life. And one of his official tasks was to read film scripts. He had to make sure that it didn´t happen a terrible mistake, as it still does nowadays. His task was easy and simply this: to make sure that Brazilian screen characters spoke Portuguese, not Spanish. Or at least that they didn´t have a Spanish accent portrayed as a Brazilian character. (Sorry, Penelope Cruz, but you in "Woman on Top" didn´t do the trick, at least not from a Brazilian artist's point of view). And it was there, at the Los Angeles effervescent scenario that he met MM.

The wealthiest Brazilian guy, a playboy, and one of the richest man on Earth at that time, with dazzling eyes to die for, and a charm that would sweep a less advised woman´s feet off the floor, made him almost like a myth. His figure was not well planned like most of the stars in the terrains where he was playing then. And yet everyone could sense that a God was emerging from a magnate, a new top guy who would circle their world with new possibilities with glory and charm, and who wanted anything else but this in that world. And how much they were thirsty for a new blood to suck on

Guinle was the real deal. He was not there for the fake of it, I mean, sake of it. He was gambling with his own life, among so many other Gables, I mean, gamblers. To tell about this kind of life, one must be pretty cool, and laid back type not to be taken by excitement. One can even become blind by all its richness and brightness.

THE MYSTERIOUS MURDER OF MM

So soon Jorginho (that´s the diminutive of his name in Portuguese and that´s how he used to be called by his family and counterparts in Brazil) starred in a real life event, having to play the character who was himself, and who had to play with so many other stars. It was indeed an epic movie shot in the hottest locations with a huge budget and an all-star cast to quote an undeniable source.

To quote only two in a surreal yet so real account, in a real life movie that he acted with Ava Gardner, "the most beautiful woman Hollywood has ever seen"; and Anita Ekberg, the La Dolce Vita star who he said of being "very unsophisticated but so beautiful — when I saw her for the first time, I almost flipped".

And to flip pages here, I won´t go much further for this suspense /mystery author is not the least interested in the lives of the rich and famous people in Hollywood, for that you have such programs as E! News, or some reality shows such as the life of the Kadarshians... exactly, who?

But to be fair, and just to show that it still touches a bit how, I will assume that MM is so close to me as if she was behind my back, reading these same words as I type them. And if I was to come up with another theory, about the six degree of separation, I would go as far as to say that I am only two degrees of separation from Marilyn Monroe, since I acted with no one less than his grandniece, Guilhermina Guinle in a Brazilian soap opera. She´s the granddaughter of Copacabana Palace Hotel´s founder. And she was as gentle and discreet to me as all of her family members were. Well, maybe not Jorginho (as they used to call Jorge Guinle). No, I didn´t meet him though, or I would be only one degree of separation from MM. And as much as I love chocolate, M&Ms with all its colors are just too much for me.

But then who is unforgettable? There she was: Marilyn, who stayed in his head his entire life… until he reached his eighty-eight years of age. Well lived then, now lived, because if you go backwards, the word "lived" means "devil". And who wants to live forever?

In 1962, Jorge went to California. He was supposed to meet Marilyn for she had promised him that she would encounter him, for he said that he would die if he didn't meet her again. And he also told her that he would be the one to take her to the Venice Film Festival. Only that she wouldn't appear for the occasion.

And the luxurious, expensive and out of this world topaz necklace that he had promised to a jeweler friend of his that he would give to Marilyn went to another neck: Jayne Mansfield's.

As much superficial and little benevolent as this might sound, there was this devastating news that of having such beauty out of his sight. And as he came back to his feet and cleared up his own sense, he frantically looked over his pocket and went after his address book to search for his next "victim" which he proudly declared of spending the next two years together.

Yet Guinle was heartbroken when he learned about the celebrity MM's death. After all, the letter J came first, and yet he had first decided for the dazzling star. So much so that he didn't take her image off of his head until recently. Even after two aneurysms.

"I have no regrets," he says. "I had a much better life than I could have imagined. I met the A to Z of Hollywood and had a great time. I might not have any money left, but, when I sleep, I dream of Marilyn." But then he died ten years ago. Would he still dream of Marilyn yet? I guess his soul didn't rest until he would be able to see this magnificent being, this light full of life and cheerful as she was, bright and spectacular on the day that he first met her when she was only twenty.

Incidentally, it was an overdose of fatigue and disgust ball that killed her.

No, I´m not talking about Marilyn now. I´m talking about another bombshell: Carmen Miranda who desperately tried to survive a life filled with mischief and sorrows that only she could explain how much misery she had to go through and how much more mystery surrounded her with her mother being sick and all; and to overcome so many obstacles to compound this tragic symphony. And she still had to play the role of a happy, sensual, sexy and exciting woman despite all the troubles that she had to go through.

She crashed several times before she could spare some time with family and friends, and be rewarded by her achievements. She even reached to the point of having gone through a series of electric shocks. And again, to be clear, I´m not talking about MM, who also had the same kind of treatments, having to be taken against her will to a therapeutically psychiatric care.

And definitely, I´m not taking it all on me, as you shouldn´t either. As I declared before, this is a work of fiction based upon facts, and any similarities with real lives... are no coincidences.

But when talking about things that sound so familiar, things that did not only happen to your neighbor but you having being through the same things that others, celebrities or not, had been, stepping in the same stones, having wearing the same hats and experiences the many pains and aches, it's like wearing their own shoes. So it is not so unusual, then it´s time to take a closer look.

For Carmen and Marilyn, they both had been taken into custody and against their will. And only those who had been through this could sense it in first person and relate to that and start putting the words out to reach more people who also had suffered in the hands of medical assistance with no clue.

No, this book is not about me. Or is it, in some way that I felt obliged to put on some light on dark matters? I´m not in any way a speculative type, but when issues like this string a cord or two inside my heart I just have to play along in the rhythm of an orchestrated scheme and open up a rainbow of possibilities and a mushroom in a blast candy-bar wrap-up to make life worthwhile. I´m as sharp and conscious as any Buddha-like figure would be in the midst of a tempest of insane acts from this crazy, frankly frantic and murky nut job that´s this world we call reality. I try to unveil the illusion that some forces in power insist on creating in order to make us sick, so that we may be as blind as a bat, battling among so many rocks in a dark cavern. Hopefully my mission here will be echoed in many findings. I just so wish for it!

When she last visited Brazil, between December 1954 and April 1955, Carmen stayed a month and a half in a self constrained diet of not seeing anyone or any words from the outside world; she spent exactly forty-nine days confined in a double suite at the hotel Copacabana Palace, by doctor's order.
She was trying to turn away from the fake image that Hollywood created of her and recover her own self, just like Marilyn Monroe in that turning point where all fame and power dissuaded them to sell their souls to the devil. They both had that charisma that one cannot fabricate but be born with and a fire in their hearts that the world outside them was eager to consume.

And in that fatidic year, in 1962, Brazilian playboy Jorge Guinle flew to the United States to give his old flame Marilyn Monroe some jewelry given to him by a friend (and his name is not revealed because first and foremost Jorginhos was a gentleman and didn´t point out names, at least not from his intimate circle). He was to accompany her to Venice for the city's film festival and wanted her to show up with some added glamour, in a beautiful topaz necklace.

Jorginho flew his way from Rio to L.A. As he so many times had made. And he walked off the aircraft when he felt a cold breeze.

"No, it is not possible!" He had a premonition that something went incredibly wrong in his attempt to come back as the epic armored or enamored shinny knight who would take his lady by the arms. He put his two feet on the ground. He looked outside the window of the limousine that would take him to the Beverly Hills Hotel.

"Can't believe she's dead!" He heard someone screaming in the short thirty-five minutes drive right there in the middle of the Rodeo Drive.

And that's when he learned about her death. No, actually, he saw it on the headlines, just like everyone else. There on the TV set where they announced Marilyn Monroe's suicide in a loop of each and every second non-stopping, so it was hard to miss.

Jorginho, although he was still called like a little boy in a sweet way, was then forty-six. And he was still a billionaire (in dollars) and amassing his fortune that he had inherited. But he was not loosing much as he was already spending so much, and still there was so much more on his shelves and under his sleeves. (I can only wonder where he would put that amount of money. Would he put all his fortune under the mattress?) And yet he was miserable, devastated.

And less than a minute later (or hours, who is counting time with that amount of cash?) he didn't freak out thinking that he had lost the battle. He called upon his white horse (or rather, his whiskey), poured it down his glass and started mumbling about whom he should call next. Who was next in his black book? His finger tip-tapped from head to bottom to arrive to the letter J. He reached his phone book; reached out to the phone in one of his luxurious five star bedrooms in the Beverly Hills Hotel, swung the rotary dial disk with one hand while holding the receiver near his ears with his shoulder. He got a ring (actually a necklace) and she answered to his call. There he had it in his hands, the necklace that he would put over the neck of the second most desirable women at that time: Jayne Mansfield in flesh and blood.

"I phoned Jayne Mansfield, who had just divorced from her husband. I wasn't able to give the jewels to Marilyn, so I gave them to Jayne. She was delighted. We spent the next two years together."

Jorginho still keeps his memories very vivid. He was not the villain of the story after all. Although his vanity would make him sound very superficial, he had a warm personality and would never portray the soul of a bad boy. He was ever too fresh and gentle for this. And yet he kept that merry-go around routine of his, as much here and as in the afterlife.

He stood there, with his head down, then looked around in a boyish manner and a little smile, while holding his right hand up.

"Pleading guilty, your honor!"

That's all that he had to say.

The blond woman took out her glasses and revealed a brownish eye embedded in a rosy secretion. She looked tired although her youthful appearance could easily disguise that she had just reached her early thirties. She put her glasses back on again and she was about to leave the Hotel´s reception hall when she remembered that she had her contact lenses in her eyes.

"Oh that's why my eyes are burning," she said to herself. "One can go blind by leaving those in."

She looked to her right and then to her left, clueless to where she could possibly be safe.

"Where is the toilet?" Misses Murphy asked the receptionist.

"On the left, near the telephone booth."

She entered the bathroom and washed her face. She looked at the mirror.

"Oh, my gosh, do I look horrible tonight!"

She then took a lipstick and passed it through her mouth like a car wash metallic broom brushing an automobile, like a vigorous brushing would do in a very resourceful and quick vehicle. She took her mobile phone that was ringing out of her bag.

"Hello?" She left her purse over the sink.

"Hi, sweetie… How is everything? How is the party?"

She looked at her watch; it was nine-eleven... PM.

"Postmortem". The word insisted on appearing in her eyes. That's how she felt anyway. She looked like a zombie and for the last few years she and her husband had been persecuted; they were in a living hell as if they were both already dead, in a post-apocalyptic state and inside a nightmare that her life had become. She couldn't believe what her friend had just told her: that she was marked to die in the same way that she had portrayed in one of what would be her last movies: in the toilet and rubbed beneath a swimming pool of blood inside a bathtub.

WHEN YOU WISH UPON A STAR

"A German ambassador was awarded the medal for Ordens Deutschen Adler, given by Adolf Hitler, for those who have served with great loyalty and diplomacy. Upon arriving in Chile's harbor city of Valparaiso the ambassador got married and had the children.

He lived a normal life, and no one would ever guess that he had been involved in the WWII, not even his family. So upon his death a big secret was kept. He left that medal to the hands of his wife who died right after him.

And the death of the eldest son who supposedly inherits the medal, not knowing about that secret kept in the back leads authorities to go after it.

But the year 1962, within the Soviet Committee that came to the World Cup, two agents were infiltrated into the team, whose goal was to retrieve the cross in the back of that medal. And right underneath the cross, a coin was hidden.

The heavy coin, the size of a penny and made of a basaltic stone with magnetite, had a triangular shape. Within its center there was a drawing encrypted, like two poles of opposite directions.

In a crescent moon shape considered to be the North Pole, there were magnetic forces that lead any other magnetic object to turn in a clockwise direction.

The South Pole on the other hand with the half-moon reflected as a relatively smaller projection with an opposite design like a mirror, leading the object in a counter-clockwise direction. Never in the human history was such an object been built. It seemed that the coin was a key that would open and close an out-of-this-world device, with a controlling force that would enrich the lives of those who touched it with psychic abilities.

In search of the coin, there were some strange deaths, occurring one in Valparaiso. Other two deaths happened right after a pilot who flew over Chile had witnessed *foo fighters*, or UFOs, non-identified flying objects in and out the area where this coin was last seen.

The two agents found out that there was some alien intelligence that was also in the look out of such key. The great secret that kept the cross and the coin was a map showing exactly where the tank was and where it kept the real treasure of Adolf Hitler.

These agents were working for Jewish magnates, belonging to a lodge with esoteric features, owners of major organizations participating in the economic and political power both for the United States.

The end of 1963 is when the hand reaches microfilm of this organization and must pass 38 years to figure out and plan the rescue of the great dome, located just below the Twin Towers.

It was believed that the U.S. government itself orchestrated and carried out the attacks in a false flag operation. This group of theories questioning the cause of the collapse of the Twin Towers had Charlie Sheen leading the claim, that it would be a controlled demolition.

Just after declaring it in an interview that he was boycotted and had his contract canceled in an important TV studio. But even before him, there came Sean Penn who was overwhelmed when he heard about the news by the direction that Politics were taken, in an imminent war against Iraq right after the September Eleven attack.

He had spent a lot of bucks, in an open letter that was published at the Washington Post and addressed to President George Bush in the Thanksgiving Sunday of 2001.

WHEN YOU WISH UPON A STAR

I remember all about it because I was there living in D.C. And I have read the whole shit, I mean, sheet. It was very depressing, actually. As if a President who after hearing about the attack became paralyzed for a second to then continue to read a book to children (if you don't remember at that time he was visiting a school when he heard about the news) would hear (or read) a man who had just played dumb in *I am Sam*. Uncle Sam wants you!

And he wants you to be strong but now Sean Penn opened a bottle of Champagne that he had bought on his way to the Cannes Festival. "Finally", he thought, "I´m not alone!"

The theorists came from all parts and defied the intelligence right when the Twin Towers collapsed. It was well known to be a conspiracy and it has even used the term inside job (internal work) to refer to the attacks in this group of theories. It has been called MIHOP an acronym meaning "Made It Happen On Purpose".

There were some gaps in the border control which lead to the access for the terrorists to attack. Those flaws in the security system and of the frontiers were later on denounced by an ex-employee of the National Security Agency, or vulgarly known as the NSA. And since then she has been banned from any type of public speech and completely discouraged to act into Politics."

"Right!" She said, after reading the files. "So now, what am I supposed to do with all this info?"

She uploaded the files and sent them to her own email account. She then wrote another message, this time to her friend:

"If something happens to me, or to my husband, you know my password..." She was about to hit the button "send" when she heard a noise right behind her back.

She looked over her shoulders and she became petrified to what she had seen. The scene of two burglars invading her house, pointing a gun into her head and taken her into custody, to then crashing into her computer was nothing comparing to what it was about to happen to her friend.

She died aged 32. Like her husband she was slowly being killed by poison. The autopsy of both bodies later on revealed that they both had a large amount of some type of metal in their hair that meaning that it took the same type of poison they use to kill rats.

2

The Church of Satan

Jayne Mansfield first got into contact with Satanism by the hands of Anton LaVey, founder of the Church of Satan. And since then she became not only a vivid follower but a livid enthusiast and avid learner of all things Satan religiosity related.

Taking a look over her handwriting and especially going through her signature, we may notice a display of enough signs of a persona worried about her public status, and so full of herself that she reveals a cross and a Christian disposition.

But almost in an antagonistic way, she revealed her thirsty for all things related to revolution, a sense of renewal, and she revels around her rebellion against traditions saying that she believes in God but she prefers a more Pagan devotion to whatever entity she thought that existed or would help her instead.

Although she almost converted to Catholicism in 1963 (and I can only suspect it was by Jorginho´s influence) and was a frequent attendee from services of the Holy Cross, the Church itself didn´t allow her to be married in the traditions, and also avoided her like the devil, such as it occurred in Ireland, for not letting her presenting her regular shows.

Pink was her favorite color. And there´s nothing new about the fact that she created a pinky dream-like state in such a fairy tale take, I mean fake, that nothing real could surpass, at least not anything from a gruesome reality. Her life was a love bubble, or something in the shapes of a gummy balloon, as she created such an artificial life, and a make believe situation where she was an eternal princess in search for love.

But there was something perverse or, at least, willing to connect with some kinky entity in her mind. When in San Francisco she went to meet the founder of the Church of Satan. There she received a medallion and the title "High Priestess of San Francisco's Church of Satan".

In her pink bedroom there is such a certified diploma of being a member of the Church framed and firmly displayed in the wall. At least for once she felt that she belonged.

No question she loved Geometry. She drew a perfect cross for such a reminder of the burden that her name would bear right in the first letter.

It was like a sign of showing how much sacrifice that she had to carry. And no wonder her signature depicts a Trapezoid.

She was constantly balancing her personal life with her external demanding struggles and her inner conflicts. And she managed to deal with that in her own way.

Although with bad influences, she had the brains to discern what was right for her. She felt like the trapezists in many situations in her life, jumping from one trapezium to the next, in a leap of faith. And I can only imagine if it was in her plans to go join another sect as she took part of the early Order of the Trapezoid that later organized the Church of Satan.

Her need for a religious faith is so openly expressed in her signature that it hurts the eyes. And there is so much more in her than meets the eyes... Notice that in her initials, the letter J gets into fusion with the M, causing an ebullient syndrome, and almost forming the universal peace symbol but with the cross more prominently showing her need for sacrifices, of her own or of others she loved; and there is a formation of the letter J with a C below. Also in her M, almost like in a shape of a heart there is this need to follow her heart and be loved, which can be translated in her need to be noticed and having so many affairs.

She also tried by all means to find the man of her dreams.

When she traces and goes such a long way to the point of outlining the letter "m" all the way up such as to meet her stylish first letter "J" she arrives to the point of saying it all <u>even</u> without saying a word.

"I need to find the man of my dreams, even if for that I will have to go through all the pains and aches of a love interest", she states. And she adds, "I will not leave my desires and my will for that, but I will go to the end of the world if needed to make my wishes come true and make ends meet."

There she also says that her life with her first husband was no piece of cake. He may be a gentleman and had treated her nicely, but the way she addresses that first letter M for Man and from her family name "Mansfield", she walks a mined field, and touches the tip of the letter J almost like carrying a cross across her numerous affairs in a most three dimensional design. I wonder if she ever thought of becoming a painter or a dress stylist. She would do great as well.

That f in the field means that she was pregnant, and to pinpoint the fact that she got married pregnant of her first husband, and as she was also very pregnant all the time (not only in the physical sense but in an intellectual way, with full of ideas, and always generating new creations).

And that she crosses the "L", in a ninety-degree angle for love, such as it was all a labor of love, she makes her inhibit this desire, as to say she didn't show half of what she came here for, her mission was much more than being a playboy rabbit, a playmate, a sex symbol. She wanted to become a myth such as Gaia, or Mother Earth, and she was indeed a Goddess of Creation. Such an unfortunate event that she died so soon. Or she would surely accomplish that goal, no doubt of that.

With her drive and wit, and her ability to make things work in her favor, she would surely reach out to the stars. And that doesn't tell about the celebrity status that she had already gained over those frantic years as a bombshell, although that could be part of her plan all along for what I mean it's in a spiritual level.

A powerful woman as she was, if and only if she had invested all the opportunity she had to make good to the world, she could have done so much more, and she had so much more to offer than that of what Hollywood made over her. And often she would disguise it in the form of alcohol and other drug-related issues that spared her of more suffering, or took her mind away from much disillusionment in a kind of escape from her own reality, to say the least.

The description over her own inscriptions goes much further: the leg of the letter y, turning into an eight (8) or the symbol of infinite, or almost like in the form an hourglass shape, which concerns to her very need of taking time by her own hands and having her over and over being concerned about her voluptuous body, and her voluminous breasts.

She was obsessively worried about her body image,

especially over her excessive body weight (after her five pregnancies, she looked round, especially from the upper body, which is emphasized in her drawing).

Also her entangled life is displayed there, with many mischief, and tricks, and meddled middle terms and so many circles and u-turns that her life had taken. Funny that she doesn't stop there, with the letter *d* almost making another circle. She says that she wanted to live her life to the fullest and didn't want it to end so abruptly.

She was killed in a car accident with her partner, the one who introduced her to the Church of Satan. That was a mysterious event. Was that an accident? It could well be, maybe. But some drivers witnessed a van following her car. Were they paparazzi trying to get a shot? Did she die in the same strange way as did Princess Di? They both were living lives to die for, when they were reaching into a sensitive spot, ruling in their own terms. Did they make enemies? Were some people pissed off by the way they lead the events surrounding them? There was a cloud of mystique and mystery hovering over their heads. Was it not an accident, but were they abruptly taken off the road to crash and burn? It was not like the case of another super star, actress and later Princess, Grace of Monaco. Both women, Jane and Diana, were killed, for they were not arguing with anyone, like Grace Kelly who knew about the risks of driving in anger and enraged she lost control over her vehicle putting not only her life but her daughter's life in risk, the latter, Stephanie, has a lucky star and who miraculously survived the tragedy. Nope. That was not the case if they were not even driving the car. They didn't have any control over the situation. They had others taking the wheel. They let the wheel of fortune decide their fate. What better excuse than fate? Jane didn't even like that word: Fate. It reminded her of Faye Dunaway, another one in the line to hate her for taking her roles in the industry, just eagerly waiting for her fatal fall. In no way they could prevent of her dying this way. Her leaving the end *d* with a lineup that shows of how committed she was to life and such a terrific gal she was, an eternal optimistic about people and circumstances. No, she could even loose her wig or suffer a scalp when the car crashed but she would never, ever surrender.

And finally, back to her signature, the way she had almost hidden the words "man" more like neglecting the *n* of "neighing" and the letter *s* from "sensuality" in her family name (borrowed from her first husband) just reveals that sex with that man was not that great anyway. So he didn´t fill her much in that field, if you know what I mean. But Paul, who divorced her almost ten years before that accident, died almost two years ago (on June 8, 2013) and he then can no longer attest if that´s true, and he wouldn't care to defend his virility and performance for all that matters.

And as much as it may appear, no, I have never met her or any one of her three husbands, although I once went to a party where William Shatner´s daughter was in. But I didn´t talk to her, I didn´t know who she was, until someone pointed her out to me. As if that would mean anything, anyway, for me she looked as ordinary as anyone else in that room. But since Mr. Shatner played a role in the movie *The Devil´s Rain* where the founder of the Church of Satan, (what was his name again?) where he worked as a technical adviser, I could nicely ask her about the many ventures in Hollywood´s golden ages. But as I´ve been always really shy, and I´m also very discreet I wouldn´t dare even staring at her.

No, I don´t know anyone related to Jayne Mansfield, not even her neat daughter who could say more about this whole ordeal, working on a TV show related to cases such as this, although I don´t think that even she could solve this mystery as her mother died in that horrible car accident when she was only five. Another lucky daughter surviving a car crash as her mother dies. Hmm, that sounds too familiar to be just coincidental...

That makes me wonder now if Grace... No, wait! Wasn't she a great friend of Frank Sinatra?? Anyway, back to Jayne's daughter, Mariska, I doubt she knew anything about her mother´s affairs, such as Stephanie knew about her fairy-tale mother, who would be an eternal Princess for the public eye. Jane was a diva. I grasped about her inner self by only reading her signature, by handwriting analysis and my formation in self-learned psychological and art studies.

Contrary to her, Marilyn Monroe and Grace Kelly who had no clue of what the opposite forces were, passed by living their lives as if they would last forever and thus becoming dead, I mean DEAF (Diamonds Enchantments Are Forever) to the risks of their surroundings and to the events what were about to come.

Jayne had a sense of better using her mesmerizing power. She knew exactly where she was stepping on, and she entered into a dimension where there was a spiritual connection with everything. She knew that one step in the wrong direction and she would be forced to vanish from the civilization, and for good. It was a cruel, ordinary world out there. And she did keep track of it. Until the day when she decided to invest too much of her time (and status) into the underworld, playing with divinities and other entities whom she was not used to manifest.

+

That altar allowed anyone to drift upon its magnitude. Any soul who would feel free enough to get hypnotized by its splendor had a need to explore its intricate weaves of a tapestry, as a trivial decoration, just like the luxurious carpets from the aristocratic Goya.

But it could also represent a surreal portrait from Salvador Dali. What embarrassed the most was that enormous sculpture in the format of a giant cone, in a somewhat phallic allusion, centered in front of the set, right above the seat of the throne.

And that was nothing compared to all the symbolism inserted in each and every image, from well dressed, sophisticated and ancient three dimensional figures, and a collection of vintage displayed side-by-side with "cachaça" and "pinga" which are two of the strongest alcoholic beverages in the world, to a cheap bric-a-brac, (or brie-a-bras) and other artificial objects considered as art by some with a composition that affected the sense of style of many, and convinced only the credulous.

As if in a dilemma, two separated and distinctive ways it was always presented in the whole celebration. It was a chaotic scene for the untrained eye. And it confused even the more habituated viewer, with huge horns in alternate pieces, the two horned adorned into "silly-gism" in which the followers (or rather, adorers) considered a divinity.

The believers are committed to the rest of their lives to accept one or another, each of which contradicts more the other. It is like a crossroad. Thus it only proposes a response to take a chance, take in a flight, and choose something between the two of them. And these are not so fine decisions, each with equally horrendous consequences, and believe in it, but being ready to pay the price for the choice one makes.

A complexity of spirituality and paganism, enriched by a gigantic wooden-made polychrome image of an African Saint, composed the whole scenario. And the mysticism evaporated its freshness by its own pores, spreading a kind of mist in the air which, nevertheless, could not disguise the unusual shadowy presence in the platform, like a spectrum of illusions. It was rather an assault to all the senses, though decency was never a necessity, being non-sense of what it was to censor.

Covered by the roughness on the surface, the sculpture's form easily betrayed the lightness and elegance of the Saint's eyes, all made of chrome. The body reflected the golden leaves which, in turn, replenished the whole ambiance with light, and all over the exquisite atmosphere, from the top to the bottom.

All the sculptures, set in a semi circle, illuminated the set with decorated wands that shivered conforming to the light that touched them, all colored and vibrant, with many rocks that scintillated and reflected the formation on the platform. An odd ordination of a clunky delight persuaded anyone less attentive to reach out to it and surrender to its power.

The Halloween conspiracy is nothing compared with what she was about to experience in a session of an exposed "dispossession" which literally means that your body was taken by a demon.

That is to say that when an evil spirit, or a bad intentioned soul possess you as a disembodied entity, sucking your magnetic field, you can even incarnate the devilish form, contaminating your body like an out of this world group of contortionists, penetrating it like invisible worms, and turning it into an ugly mess, I mean, mass... and you don't even know it is all happening to you or to someone else, something takes control over your body.

It dominates you in such a way that you are now a believer. But others will take you to a session to release that force away from you. Where all that come from it? Please, I am still trying to explain why she was even there! She needed magic in her life. And she was hungering for an exotic scene to worship. She was eagerly waiting to contemplating an ocean of love. Only that the red sea of love that she was about to swim would be surrounded by blood. And she was willing to give up her soul in order to accomplish that.

In February 1958, three years after been first displayed as the playmate of the month in Playboy's magazine Jane Mansfield was stripped to her waist in a *Mardis Grass* party in Brazil.

Mansfield and Mickey Hargitay attended a dance at Copacabana Palace Hotel. Jayne wore a very small dress with flowers all sewed on the bodice. As if possessed Jayne stood up in her chair and started to shimmy her whole body, until her companions were so excited that they pulled the flowers off her chest and made her appear nude, as in a topless. They had her stripped to her waist and they in turn pinched her so hard she had bruises all over her chest. She seemed to enjoy the whole ordeal and it did indeed look like it was the deal. She looked as if she was in a trance. Mickey pulled her down and covered her with his coat.

They suddenly broke out of the party and left the ballroom to take a limousine and headed up north to go to another party, in a more underground fashion way by striptease dancer Luz del

Fuego naturist club's Sun Island at the Bay of Guanabara. Jayne and her husband arrived in their motor launch as Luz and a companion were bathing naked in the sun. Luz and her companion friendly approached the visitors, and they gently said that they were more than welcomed to make a tour in the island as long as they left their pudency (and prudency) out. Although Jayne said she would like very much to see the island which was covered by a luxurious forest, she seemed to be hesitant. Luz del Fuego with her hot temper and her imperative demands with a fuzz covering her body with her luxurious black hair like Eve, and made a fuss out of what later would become the news of not only gossip magazines but serious newspaper at that time.

"Only nudists are allowed on this beach, bitch!" She repeated. Well, not the bitch part, for she was classy and very polite, she had been raised well enough as not to say a bad word.

"No clothes, no blows, only pros... she naturally glows!" Her friend said looking at his divine brunette partner.

"Now that's a grit grater, I mean great greeter!" Jayne answered jumping off the boat. They went to the pier. Mickey was already throwing all his clothes off and put his ego away as he went out of sight, jumping into the warm water.

But when asked by Luz to strip her clothes off, Jayne oddly refused to disrobe completely as it was the rule to visitors who came to the island and then the couple left as they were forbidden to enter there. It seemed too much for Jayne to "bare". Bear in mind that she had always been paid to show off her parts. Her modesty barred her visit to the nudist colony. Luz del Fuego complained that Jayne was implying that nudity was immoral.

"Too bad I'm not Marilyn Monroe, she is a naturalist." Jayne said that with a bit of a sarcastic spit.

"I would not feel right..." She then replied to Luz.

"I won't strip me off and I'm so sorry about that!"

"That volcano erupting like a bombshell in the sea of hypocrisy thinks she could break up my own rules and play all "no see on the sea". Was she sorry, all right?"

And Luz del Fuego quoted her later on to the journalists. An island visited by international celebrities on the likes of Brigitte Bardot and Steve McQueen. Although McQueen, who had so many worldwide friends, so much so that he was the only celebrity to carry the Bruce Lee´s casket in 1973. He was a frequent visitor of the island. But once he woke up with a creepy snake rolled around his neck, and other insects which were all crawled over his body, he never came back since then. But he was used to this near death experiences, as he was next in the list of celebrities to be murdered by the Masons family, which included in their morbid agenda the actors Burt Lancaster and Elizabeth Taylor. But luckily the members of that sect were captured in 1969 after killing in cold blood and a brutal way Sharon Tate in her eight-month pregnancy.

Back to the sunny hot island with temperatures reaching over one hundred degrees Fahrenheit or 40 degrees Celsius, Jayne´s refusal had only ignited more fire on Luz´s tongue that spitted fire like a serpent. Funny enough, for moral purposes, besides clothes, alcohol beverage and sex practices as well as swearing language and profanities were forbidden in the island.

"But showing off her boobs in a cleavage-baring, barely provocative pose in a too tempting way to get attention to her breasts and her nipples falling on her plate while seated on the table next to Sophia Loren in a Beverly Hills party was not much to ask", grasped Luz del Fuego going back to bake in the sun of her Sun Island.

Jayne and her husband then left back to Rio. But before that Mickey went back to the beach. He had no problems showing how so strong and powerful he was. Finally, as it was already dark when he came back to the boat, he saw a distressed Jayne. She was there, crying out all wondering if he would ever come back from that paradisiacal island.

"You had to see it, I couldn't believe it myself have I not seen this through my own eyes... there were birds everywhere with unimaginable beauty out there, all singing their own songs... Lizards so well-developed they look like alligators. And crocodiles so huge they looked like dragons. And many other reptiles so big they all looked like dinosaurs..." He was mesmerized by what he had experienced.

"And why do you look so sour... Are you still sober?" To portraying a life as a Tarzan and Jane in an exotic island had always been their dream. But it seemed that for an urban Jayne, used to the artificial spotlight and not the natural sun, only burned her peroxide scalp.

They were both very athletic, but Jayne always had a weakness to too much drinking which caused her Hungarian and more healthier-inclined hubby to having pretending he was blind in more than many occasions.

"Too many rules in Paradise", she replied. "Besides, no alcohol and no sex, that's indeed too much to ask!"

Mickey didn't pay much attention to his newly-wed wife and much less to what she said in despite of all her humiliation. After making him prove his love for her, by having to build a swimming pool in the shape of a heart before she decided that he was good enough to marry her, he didn't know what else he could do for her, to make her happier. She was certainly really mad at his attitude of leaving her all by herself and waiting for him, and afraid of being attacked by a monkey or other sea creatures. But he didn't quite get what was going on in her brain.

He hopped in the boat just hoping she wouldn't complain much in their way back to the hotel. But as she kept saying how hard it was to stay there in that hot sun and frying her brains out, he started to get pretty cynical about the whole situation. He just made some mockery about the entire ordeal.

"Why did you come here, in the first place?" He said angrily. "Weren't we supposed to have much fun?"

"Yes, but I meant it together... not only fun for you."

"So you are implying that I do not care for you, that I'm cynical and selfish... is that what you are trying to say?"

"No, you misinterpreted me. I really want a tour in the Island." Jayne tried to cool her husband down a little as she saw that she was swimming in hot water.

"Oh, so would you like a tour now?" Then he turned the boat side by side and went on making a tour bouncing back and forth, accelerating, making waves and leaving the boat in circles for hours, right there in the middle of the ocean.

"Mickey, honey, would you please stop that? I'm getting really sick..." The blond bombshell tripped into the lifeboat inside the barge. She was about to throw the beverage that she just had in her stomach over that shaking boat. She curled over and looked pale. It was a rough sea and scene.

"Didn't you want a trip in the island? There you have it!"

"Why are you being so rude? Why do you have to be so mean to me like that? I didn't do anything..."

"Exactly! You just stayed there... but I did have some fun, and that's why you are so angry with me?"

"No, darling, I don't mean that. I just thought we could both have some fun... that's all!" She thought that she was being the nicest person in the world... So why in heaven's he would be so retarded to treat her like a bag of garbage. But he only heard her whining over her wine. This way she would never win.

The more she complained the more he accelerated the fast boat. And oh, man, he was fast! Speed racer (or "arsed") was his second name anyway.

Jayne fell back again. As the launch turned and Mickey made a zigzag movement around the bay, Luz del Fuego could swear that this was just a play as she saw the whole show from the beach, and Jayne coming up and down like she was practicing for a dance presentation.

"See you next fall!" Luz greeted to Mickey, as he waved back for he had already promised her that he would be back to that Paradise, making sure that his next time he would come alone. And there Jayne felt the pain and fell once more.

So mysteriously are the ways that things happen in life, we cannot quite understand how and why the events following with enough coincidental points are presented with such lack of discrepancy, that they can only become myths. Those two daring women died in the same year of 1967: Jayne on June 29 (and with something related to the Goddess Juno) and Luz del Fuego on July 19, tragically murdered by a fisherman who she was about to denounce and he would surely be condemned for overfishing only if she had survived to tell the tale.

Mickey was possessed by his own sense of virility. His eyes turned to a reddish flash as he crossed the Atlantic Ocean.

And that was the same image recorded in my mind when I heard about a kind of shaman being possessed by an energy, his eyes turning into red, and he swirling his body around and spinning in and out like a dervish (or like a devilish being, I dare say) and who was doing his best performance in the terrain of *Macumba* in Rio de Janeiro.

It's all a folkloric view: Chicken loose heads, people drink just a little too much and not only from an alcoholic source, as much as from blood. Women and men dance almost naked, all night and day. They sing and dance frenetically around the fire. And she could hear a cry.

A girl possessed by an evil spirit just fainted on the floor in the middle of the circle.

She thinks that she was overwhelmed by that session, the lack of oxygen, along with the intoxicating smoke from the fire, and with the entire circle to making they lose their senses, and giving them the total freedom for a contact with the darker sides of their souls.

A woman dances freely, a snake surrounding her body. She bounces back and forth and touches the image of a saint, shaking it and dancing, as if it was an animated character. *Yemanja*, the queen of the ocean is taken from the altar. They threw her at the sea, with white candles over her figure.

She then hears another cry in the night from a ghetto of Rio. Now it is not the girl but the whole ceremony is varnished by demons.

It is a tribal ritual that she will never forget. They danced in circle, and they all slithered their bodies in a rainbow shower with a colored wheel of ecstasies, all in trance. The sun came to show its immaculate face at the Copacabana Beach and the boys played *Capoeira,* traditional Brazilian moves and rhythms, a mixture of dance and martial arts on the sand; the whole group encircled them, pivoting not as a group but as an unique soul, chanting strange names while playing the vibrating instrument made of wood called Berimbau. She walks and she feels dizzy just by looking down, immersed on the zigzags from the sidewalks all embodied with the Burle Marx's ingenious moves, of a rather sinuous design.

A man looks into her eyes. He looks intensely at her. Or I should say, he looks through her eyes. She felt so transparent that she fell down on his spell. Forgive me but this vibe requested another rhyme: "She feels the smell, and she fell over his spell..."

It seems that he is the devil himself, impersonated in a well-shaped human form, or he is the evil spirit who had just left the girl's body and tried to possess her. And she sees that it is not his eyes that see hers, but someone else is seeing through her eyes that look back through her. She starts to shiver.

She wants to leave the place, but he takes her and he starts to dance with her back touching his belly slightly against her, spraying his sweaty body all over her skin. Suddenly she sees many hands touching her body, wanting her possessed in what I call a total freaky Halloween.

Her hips swing, following the rhythm in a sequence of an almost choreographic movement coming from the sound of the bongos.

She first hesitates. Then she leaves her whole body bouncing, while she allows herself to take part of this. A strong sound so deeply inside her ears, in a symbiotic war of flesh and lust matches with her heart beatings. She loosens up and gives herself permission to lose control to their souls.

Now she is one of them, there is just no way back. Little would she know, and she would learn then that she had already lost all of herself. All is black.

She faints. They take her to the bathroom. They then take some fresh water from the sink and start to throw the liquid over her face. She comes back to her senses and starts to cry. They left her alone.

They were expecting the blond to get out of that toilet soon. Another woman with sunglasses was inside there too. She left before the blond. They kidnapped her instead.

One of the bad guys had a knife in his hand.

"She is no billionaire's wife!"

They grabbed her arm, and as they walked at the Hotel's entrance, a man passed. She looked at him trying to make eye contact. In a desperate move she held his arm firmly.

"Call the police!" She shouted. The kidnappers left the Hotel with the blond. But the receptionist saw when they left with the victim, and after a rapid chasing them by the police officers, one of them jumped out of the car. The other two couldn't hold her anymore and they were caught into their own equivocal plot.

$$3$$

Mind Control and the Beta Program

Everything in the room is WHITE.

In fact I can't even see anyone just white objects -

They cut me open

Like out of a raggedy ann doll—is given up—
Arthur is disappointed—
let down.

Out of control from the mind program, Marilyn was taken by *spy-chiatrists (*yes, I know, I don't have dyslexia anymore, only when I was a child and I didn't misspell it wrongly. It was just wordplay among so many pranks and played stuff rolling over this statement) as she was found dead just after the following public event:

On May 19, 1962 after hearing Marilyn singing to him the most sensuous "Happy Birthday" from the world History JFK confessed and declared as not to forfeit such state of grace:

"I can now retire from politics after having had 'Happy Birthday' sung to me in such a sweet, wholesome way;"

And a year later he indeed did retire, or rather was forced through to get a retirement and he was about to break into a long, dreadful, forceful rest.

The Strenuous Life and Death of some Anna Nicole a.k.a. Marilyn Monroe Wannabe and who was compared to Jayne Mansfield. On February, 2007 she was found dead in a hotel room in Hollywood, Florida.

There are so many lies out there that the truth itself seems a bit like a piece of theater, a soap opera and a work of fiction. But as many films and soaps and other literary works had already portrayed, it´s not art that imitates life, or that reality is reflected upon fictional events. Instead what´s real in fact always seems to overwhelm even the most imaginative and ingenious minds. And so it was the case with the wannabe starlet Anna Nicole.

She was born Vickie Lynn Hogan, and if you are the least concerned about mind control programs you know that the first thing to take someone out of one's reality and make a fictional characters out of someone own life is to change the original name. Because that´s what they did with Marilyn Monroe, to whom they first changed her original name to Mona (or Monarch, like saying "My Ark", as an analogy to the ark of covenant, or convenience, an allusion to all the treasure and the money that they could make out of her. A Monarch is what they call those who are hypnotized to make good service. And there are still so many more of other personalities who serve them as well that it´s hard to keep track of them all.

After a slip as a stripper in Houston, Texas, she finally ended up being in Playboy magazine and became Hugh Hefner´s protégée. And it was then that she became so brainwashed to wanting to become the next Marilyn Monroe.

The director Stanley Kubrick tried many times to open up people's minds with his films. And what would turn out to be his last movie, *Eyes Wide Shut,* I rather say *Open,* based upon Arthur Schnitzler 1926's fiction *Dream Story* (really?) he showed more in the cutting scenes than from anything else portrayed in the final cut. In the end he died six days after screening his final cut and being miserable by the editing result. Or was he killed to not screen his film fully the way that he had planned to show the underworld and denounce people in his own metier meter by meter?

The Strange Case of Brittany Murphy

Back in the year 2009, another starlet, "dumb" or also playing as such, a blond bombshell was found dead in her house's bathroom. Again they accused her on being a drug addicted, and she accused them on this foul play, vindicated case of fabricating such lies just to have her dead and never be convicted of her murder.

Her husband told a friend about his worries of the couple having been under surveillance, and had her phone bugged. And in the same way that it came to his acknowledging about this, actually, soon after that he was found dead on the same mysterious way as his endearing wife Brittany. And such as it was the case for Marilyn Monroe when she told about the threats that she had been through, confining her fears to her doctors and her close friends, and even to the press and other people thinking they were crazy and on drugs to speak about those paranoid events. A few months later, on December 21, Brittany was found dead. She was only 32. Even their ages were so close together. Marilyn died at age 36.

That would open another can of worms saying that those two deaths were too coincidental and too close to each other where she was allegedly under the lenses of the US Home Security watch list. And that would only make the case even more mysterious; only if she was still alive to tell the facts.

I guess she was not even able to defend herself when she tried to support her friend Julia Davis. That she wouldn't be capable of knowing what or who actually killed her. I cannot hear her voicing about it, that's such an eerie way to say that. As crazy as it sounds, I'm not the least able to channel her thoughts here.

"Hello, Brittany... Earth calling!"

Nope. No answer.

Wherever she might be now, so that she and her husband who died just a few months later in the strange same way, they both could not rest in peace. Or just to quote her faithful friend Julia Davis, "Brittany wasn't a junkie, she wasn't a party girl. She was a sweet, innocent young woman... She didn't deserve to die at such a young age." And so it goes for Marilyn Monroe.

All these stories have some points in common: bombshells bursting out of their lives by drug abuses. But let's face it: Are they really responsible for that? Apart from being murdered... even Anna Nicole who had homicide, suicide and natural causes abolished from her medical file) still could be seen as a case of murder.

If you don't take the many conspiracy theories like revolving doors, running around so many facts and disturbances hovering over those amazingly beautiful and astonishing, intelligent women, so smart that they disguised their high IQ to play dumb, although both genuinely ingenious AND ingenuous, you cannot discard the passivity of a foul play. No, I do not think Anna Nicole was being vigilant (maybe only on her weight) and she was under surveillance even though she became protagonist of her own reality show. But if you believe in mind control program and that Marilyn Monroe was a Beta program, the first mind controlled bombshell in the entertainment industry, she who actually was very controlled by her own doctors, would have being a success unless she didn't start to become paranoid (or not) to believe that she was being followed in each and every step that she would make. And she did indeed state that she would be a whistle-blower of some of the actions where she was the pivotal target.

And then a curse takes its course and we can only concord and indorse it in homeopathic doses...

Another star, although from the Martial Arts, also had some martial laws running through his brain. He apparently suffered a course, which went back to his own father being killed in a strange way.

Bruce Lee also had the same prognostic: his taking pills to distract a current headache lead to his death after a mix up of other medications. But even after so many years, things are not conclusive in his case. Was he murdered by the Chinese Mafia which was enraged by his teachings of Kung Fu to the Western World?

Lee was working in the studio on his new film *Enter the Dragon*. His head was hot, he felt like it would explode with all the aches and pains and breaks he had gone through to the final synchronizations of the film. Plus they had turned off the fan in the studio for the noise was too loud and that it would eventually distract the playing of the action. He then went to a break to go wash his face in the toilet.

When he went down on his knees to try finding his contact lenses that he had allegedly said to have dropped after almost collapsing, a colleague came abruptly towards him to check if he was feeling all right. He was a strong man, hard to die and he would never convince himself that he was sick. He got up saying that he was fine and ready to go back to work.

It was then that a few minutes later, back on the studio he did feel a cold electric current flowing through his system and reaching out to his brain. He shivered and later on he collapsed and they took him to the hospital. He became unconscious. He was not responding to any words. He had convulsions.

Was that part of that Chinese curse that ran through his family? Or did someone just give him some substance, the way they did to Jayne in that crazy ritualistic party that they had her collapsing in the bathroom floor? It was then that Bruce knew about the dangers that his own family was to be part of did he not take matters to his hands.

Still at the hospital bed, Linda came beside him, and after one hour and half he woke up from the trance and it was then that she heard him speaking which was apparently pure gibberish. He decided to tell his wife about the vision he had while convulsing and said that he had seen two tombs: one was written his name and just beside that there was the name of his son, Brandon Lee.

"Are you sure you saw the dates right?" Linda then asked him, believing in him one hundred percent. She always respected and never took for granted his suppositions and some would even question if they were only superstitions.

"Yes, I'm definitely positive I will die sooner, but I still can change this. Let there be only a tomb for Brandon Bruce Lee, not his body. The date was 1993. They shall take his name, but not take his soul; I am sure I will die soon. But please don't let them take our son from you. Please make sure you will leave his tomb next to mine. But only a black stone."

Later on, doctors diagnosed him of having convulsions though due to unknown causes for he had a perfect health.

After feeling really sick, a friend offered Bruce Lee a medication that she often took while feeling headaches. This seemed to be fatal in the end.

I'm not here to speculate on the causes of his death, but only to realize about his entire legacy, his films, his Martial Art, his methods of fighting, his moves and movies and his life. But one thing that I feel it is true, and is that he's very much alive in spirit, after visiting his grave four months ago, that being on September, 7 2014. And right when I passed through his grave and seated on the cement bench before it I was feeling a warmth in my hand while meditating in front of his tomb: His soul is still so much alive, and full of colors, as much as his own son.

When I was walking towards his grave two men were descending their way out, going down towards the main gate of the place where Lee was buried, at the Lakeview Cemetery in Seattle. One of them looked at me as I went up and he went down his way and we came to cross paths. He was a *chatain clair*, which in French means that he had a light brownish hair.

And he wore glasses. I sensed that he had some Martial Arts training, being myself a Kung Fu golden belt trained by an accomplished and important, recognized master *sifu* in America. We didn't speak but I knew that he was somehow related to the Lee's legacy.

Now people so fanatic for the conspiracy theories are just recently investigating the similarities of traces saying that Christopher Greene (The AM reporter and activist, the king of conspiracy theories break down) is actually Brandon Lee who faked his own death. Maybe it was all planned by his own father prior to his death, and her wife having promised him that she would take such a good care of him, as to not allowing his son to die the date that Bruce saw in his vision. So, it was all played out to distract him from the public view. Or was that a foul play to make the movie where the supposedly fatal shooting happened in "The Raven" sells more? (It was actually called *The Crow*, but this is still fiction based upon facts, so let's keep it like that).

All those are intriguing questions like unsolved mysterious and they would keep distracting and puzzle their fans maybe for the rest of their lives.

During the Independence Day in Brazil, and there I was, paying tribute to The Greatest Movie Fighter Ever.

As I seated before his grave I felt my hands very warm, and then I bowed in respect for what he represented to me since I was a little girl when I watched his films and tried to imitate his moves.

Later on I became a martial artist myself, practicing Tai Chi and Chi Kung, and then obtaining my degree in Kung Fu when I went to study with a *sifu* (High Master) at the US Martial Arts Academy in Gaithersburg, Maryland where I got my golden belt. All that started with a star that had influenced me beyond his imagination.

I took two pictures of his grave and a multicolored light appeared to be coming from the stone which bears his name and the rays almost touched the soil coming towards me.

I took that as a token for his appreciation of me going there.

For me it was just a sign saying that he was really grateful for my effort of coming all the way up there to make a reverence towards him. And then I asked him to give me an advice. And when I asked if I should follow his steps, already leaving his grave's spot, I felt a creative energy embodying me and then I had a certainty touching right through the core and in my entire soul.

"Keep doing what you are doing. You are fine. Keep walking in your own way." Those are the words I heard from him.

A ray of light travels through the whole picture and lies down on earth as a blessing coming from the sky. The touch of the sun makes a trail and surrounds the statue of Christ the Redeemer in the Corcovado Mountain in Rio.

The Sugar Loaf embraces the Copacabana Beach with her sweet arms covering the eternal blue sky. The desert made of sand and erosion from the deforestation of the mountain by people who surround the "Rocinha", the most famous "favela" or slum located in Rio de Janeiro, which plans to wake up late in the laziness of the slow-motion days, could easily be explained by the latest incidents.

Two more policemen were killed while trying to penetrate its intricate drug dealer's fighting gang jungle.

There she lives, Christy, like crucified in another cross, but this being the diminutive of her name which is Christina.

She lives alone, her mother died of cancer when she was fifteen. And her father, according to her mother, he never existed. It was as simple as that.

Pointless to ask about more, only that her mother was a Latina, yet American woman as well, since America includes both North and South Hemisphere. "We are all Americans!"

Christina is a mulatta, with her gray and greenish eyes and curly blond hair that drops like silky stars in the ocean and falls over her shoulders, so abundant it covers half of her chest, a cascade that stops only by touching the middle of her back.

She looked like a *Yemanja* figure portrayed by many covered with a blue cape filled with stars and a half moon over her forehead.

MIND CONTROL AND BETA PROGRAM

Christina works at the factory in the Ipanema Beach, near the street called upon the name of the famous composer Vinicius de Moraes.

Vinicius, though not as famous as his companion, co-wrote the song "Girl from Ipanema" with Mr. Tom Jobim, who died few years ago in the city that he adopted as his home: New York.

She also has a boyfriend. But his character is so full of complexity and misty desires that it can be easily matched up with the whole Copacabana scenario. He indeed presents himself as a "not a nice person" or a bad boy just like the designs in his shorts. And that gives him a mystique, flair, also to frighten people around.

He goes by the motto: "If you mess with me, you are playing with fire!" And he enjoys this frightening atmosphere, this scaring aura that he mathematically creates around himself.

His mother seemed to have created a monster out of her own child. And Christina knows that.

Although all the missives by the police department and people around telling her to stay away from him, she wants to change that Karma.

She wants to make him the perfect guy, her prince charming, and she believes she can do that. Like all dreamers she believes in a perfect future where she will be able to surpass all obstacles and live in serenity.

She really believes that. She knows that he is not that bad guy after all. She also knows that he gives her money to go to school, although she knows very well where this money come from, she never speculates or talk about this.

And she is happy that she can complete her studies. Otherwise, she would be doomed to live forever earning less and spending more than her money could afford.

When those two souls, the girl from the Ipanema Beach and the girl from the "Quaker's Preach", would finally encounter each other? When those parallel lives would find a crossroad? If they live in parallel that would mean that they never will.

But they've got a connection. And here is where all lives can be the same, all lived, although not exactly "lived" or delivered, as in Latin "libertas" as a liberated state. And I wonder if there is something to do with "Lieber" from German, and I guess that's for Liberty, as if all love is free. But at least, they are the same characters in exactly the same plot.

Christina has a famous friend, considered a celebrity in her own country. And this friend of hers works for GBO Network, an enterprise in Brazil that owns many companies including the most famous TV Station in Brazil.

Her friend works as an actress, and she works in a Soap Opera that is about to finish in a week. She meets her friend, Christina, at night, after both go out of their work time. They talk about trivial things. They go out to dance, and "have fun", as they both say to each other. And they are both nineteen years old. They have so much in common...

Christina also wants to become an actress and she had just started at the University of Rio de Janeiro, the "URJ", since her boyfriend decided to help her to invest on her dream.

"Oh, it is so urgent that you finish the 'URJ', girl!"

"Yes, I know, the URJ so urge me to do that too!" She replied to her famous friend.

That is the advice of Cindy to her friend. Cynthia's mother is a writer and she is the one writing the story for the Soap Opera where her daughter participates as one of the principal characters.

Although Christina has a boyfriend who gives her his support, he is a violent man, a "mucho" macho type of guy.

She talks so little about him, although never belittles him, not so much for the lack of opportunity but more as an embarrassment by the way that he treats her.

Cindy has the most marvelous man in the world. He is rich. He is famous and has the most wonderful smile someone would ever desire to look at when feeling sad. He would lighten up the most miserable of souls. He had also a superb personality and he could be easily described as the man of any girl's dream. He was indeed a dream. Sometimes Cindy seemed to be so fragile, so vulnerable, that she looked more like a pigeon crying as she spoke about her dreamy life.

"You know, Chris, I love this man," she says to her friend, feeling so insecure and sobbing throughout the whole sentence. "Sometimes I am afraid to lose him. He is so gorgeous and there are just too many women running around him, and drilling their way towards him, drooling all over his body!"

"Imagine, you, afraid of losing him?"

"Yeah, sometimes I just start to wonder if that is not too much for me...you know, like that saying: it is too good to be true..."

"Oh, don't be silly, girl! He loves you so much that nothing would ever separate you two, nothing would make you apart f4rom each other. Nothing! I could not imagine Roy leaving you, never!"

"...Till death shall do apart..." she said, with a sad regard.

She kissed her friend good-bye, and she disappeared between the crowds at the Copacabana Avenue. She looked down and she got dizzy by the stripes that make the way with little pieces of tiles that decorate the sidewalk of the famous beach.

The night was clear; the moonlit embraced the Ocean, where so many times they would bathe themselves up to release their hot bodies from the high temperatures.

The tropical breeze filled her lungs with a nice sensation, as if a divine beverage touched her whole body. She drank the sky and she kissed the moon. It is time to go back home.

She turned to see her friend, but Cindy was already gone.

She quickly arrives at the *Rocinha*. Some eyes follow her to reassure that she is a recognizable face. She waves her hand. One of the guys had a gun in his hand. The other next to him waves back to her.

"Hello, sweetie!"

She enters into what she calls her palace: a couple of walls made of wood, and the rest made of hard paper. She reflects herself at the mirror on a small part of the wall where a brick supports a piece of wood that is fallen apart: she is the queen on her ordinary life, but she dreams of living over an imaginary world.

"Soon I will become an actress, and this whole scenario will have turned into memories of a bad dream. Soon, I will become famous and the whole world will know my name!"

The next day, she hears the news, and she hangs her head out like trying to take it off of her neck, and forcing it against her chin.

"Wasn't she your friend, Christy?" asks her neighbor, a round woman, in her late fifties with her beautiful round eyes so afflicted dancing one side to the other and all around their orbits. She seemed so excited, almost happy, jumping across the fence that separated their worlds, eager to tell her the news.

Christy doesn't talk. Her friend was dead, victim of a violent murder. What it seems like a routine in the faceless *favelas*, for her would be the most dreadful news that she could receive.

"And I was with her the night of her murder..." she thinks, and she collapses in tears.

Savage hands cruelly killed Cindy. What first appeared to be a case of a satanic ritual was more like an act of savagery. Her neck totally injured, with many cuts, as if she was sacrificed to death, was showed in a sequence of photos running out like a cat chasing his food in the newspaper of the entire country.

Who would kill such a nice girl? She was such a beauty full of life. To kill someone who was closer to being an angel?

Apparently, after she talked to Christy, and was walking back to her house, she met a man in a bar at the corner of Copacabana Avenue.

He had some bad habits, with his rude look and weird manners; some could even say that he looked a lot like a James Dean type of guy. And his pants looked dirty. He was a worker of a "Metallurgic city" in a village near the beach of Angra dos Reis, some two hundred miles away from Rio.

This guy used to play cards every afternoon taking his beer over his mouth, sipping on it as simultaneously as he grabbed a card. He was there near the beach with his friends when he met her.

He offered her to ride back to her house. Cindy accepted it, since it was getting late and she wanted to be back before her husband, to prepare him a nice dinner. And then, his wife, who was three months pregnant, saw them both together, and in an act of jealousy she came to her throat. Cindy tried to defend herself and hit the pregnant woman hard. She had beaten her twice in her swollen stomach. Her husband seeing the whole scene tried to protect his wife and took Cindy by the throat. He suffocated her.

The woman then grabbed a knife in her purse and inserted the sharp instrument over her neck as many times as her hands could possibly manage to do. She was so infuriated with the scene of her own man around with another woman that her husband couldn't stop her from that insane act.

So, what first seemed like a sacrifice for a bloody ritual was actually an act of insanity from a woman who lost her head.

But to uncover the murder, for his wife's innocence, and later regret, he took the body of the young woman and put on his trunk.

So that they could not pledge her guilty, he left the actress's body on the road and he went back home with his wife. But the media covered the crime so well, that the husband wasn't able to cover up for her. Being an actress from that major channel helped not to dissolve the mistakes but they did solve the mystery over her cruel assassination almost immediately after it occurred and the perpetrators had to no other alternative and they finally revealed the truth.

Otherwise this investigation could have taken months, if not years to be solved. If not for the hard work of both policemen and reporters who actually helped find the suspects by asking questions to some eyewitnesses, it would be even harder for a mother to go on with her life after this dreadful tragedy.

Cindy's mother would still be in such a shock state, that she wouldn't have found the strength to write another script in her remaining life. If you could call that a life: wasn't the murder of her only daughter a sentence for her own soul's death? Only after twenty years that had passed like a living nightmare that her mother would be able to grab a pen and write again.

Christina was desolated. Her friend was so endearing to her that she imagined her as if she was still alive.

"Cindy!" she said and smiled. The now imaginative friend lightened up there by her side, as she walked in the streets of Rio during the nights of shinning eyes.

She looked at the moon and she could imagine her friend smiling back at her, to seeing Cynthia's face, brightening up her day with a white full moon flair and so darling and divine she could feel her touching her soul, spreading her veil of naive dreams through the night.

But the days were always gray now for Christina. And she decided that she didn't want to become an actress after all. She just wanted to be closer to her friend and now this dream was also gone. Or not.

And that is when the lives of both Christy and Christie meet. They were both mourning the death of a silent soul. They both decided to give up their lives for the sake of a beloved one.

Christina gave up her dream for her friend, and Christie gave up her own life.

"The key to immortality is first living a life worth remembering."

Bruce and Brando Lee graves at the top of the mountain in the Lakeview Cemetery in Seattle the day I visited him and he came to see me by channeling in a dazzling evening with a rainbow made of splendorous rays of light.

4

UNITED ARTISTS

Hannah, can you hear me? Wherever you are, look up Hannah! The clouds are lifting! The sun is breaking through! We are coming out of the darkness into the light! We are coming into a new world; a kindlier world, where men will rise above their hate, their greed, and brutality. Look up, Hannah! The soul of man has been given wings and at last he is beginning to fly. He is flying into the rainbow! Into the light of hope, into the future! The glorious future that belongs to you, to me and to all of us. Look up, Hannah. Look up!

(The final speech from *The Great Dictator*)

D.W. Griffith, Mary Pickford, Charlie Chaplin (seated) and Douglas Fairbanks at the signing of the contract establishing United Artists motion picture studio in 1919. Lawyers Albert Banzhaf (left) and Dennis F. O'Brien (right) stand in the background. Charles Chaplin was a character by himself, as he became detached from real life and turned into a cartoon.

"Man as an individual is a genius. But men in the mass form the headless monster, a great, brutish idiot that goes where prodded."

"LUCKY" IN THE SKY WITH DIAMONDS

UNITED ARTISTS

When Charles Chaplin founded the United Artist he was establishing a financial freedom and the distribution of more independent films opening up a whole new world for all artists in Hollywood. His speech could well resemble the idea of getting rid of the greed and oppression among those who wanted to guarantee whole rights over the cleverest, dearest and most well thought creations.

As much as they were ingenious they were not so ingenuous, so naïve and they knew they were being taken advantage of their efforts and getting too little from their own work. The big industry was already implanted back then. It was only a matter of time on how much bigger than that it would become to swallow their creators.

Then in 1940 United Artists was not able to keep up and stand in their own feet as they were losing money making only mediocre moves and movies that left audiences wanting to leave the theaters and turning on their TV sets. It was a defeated battle. To go against the control system was like swimming against the flow. They gave up trying to establish a fair business and started a different approach in the industry.

After all it was the future of the Cinema that was at stake. Not their lives, but their creations. And their creations were their babies which they carried in their own hands. Nothing easy to let some sloppy nannies take care of their business.

Studios started to pop up, competition was harsh, no one seemed to care or to help much one another. It was one for all, and let all the others run their own buzz. And yet the anti-trust speech was working somehow.

Chaplin managed to keep up a good deal of freedom from his own movies. Although apparently he had the cake and ate it too, things were not so smoothly accomplished as the viewer's empty chairs in the theaters seemed like a plague to be avoided at all costs. And as the audience of their movies was becoming rather scarce resource he was obliged to shoot ad aim other targets.

And yet again they had to convey into another plan or strategic move. So they gave up to the small tube and let TV run the shows, starring new TV shows and programs of all kinds. This opened up a new venue for all lives concerned. That's when *I Love Lucy,* a popular show even today was brought to you by such an independent and ebullient red-haired artist and former ballerina, Lucille Ball. But of course she couldn't make such a big success by her, alone. Many gifted writers and producers were among those who gave Lucille a ball.

But like it or not, *Some Like it Hot.* After all, to quote Tony Curtis, "kissing Hitler" was not such a bad idea. Of course, he said it to be a joke. Like saying that Marilyn was so hot, like the fires of hell! Well, nobody is perfect! He was also in the list as the bombshell's lover back in the late 1940s. And if it's compared to him and the United Artist that produce the movie's with its $500,000 still couldn't reach her goals and gold.

Marilyn Monroe alone got her teeth in the package earning $800,000, a precedent among producers and by such making a fuss. After all, marketing is the biggest office box attracting tractor. And *Diamonds Are Forever.* Though later *The Misfits* didn't fit the protocol, becoming a financial fiasco and making Marilyn loose her assessment and consequently her inconsistent and inconsequential life.

Back to our days...

Good news: Kids on the Block! The Pakistani activist of the rights for girls to have education, Malala Yousafzai, has recently won the Nobel Prize, being the youngest to receive the prize and giving hope over the gender inequality that hover over women around the world.

In her speech at the Commonwealth Day in March of this year she says, "Dear sisters and brothers, in this world, we are living as family of nations and it is necessary that each member of this family receives equal opportunities of economical, social and especially educational growth. Even if one member stays behind, the rest can never go forward."

Malala was shot for defying the authority in a kind of censorship political effort to ban females to attend school. They are afraid women can be part of social and political activities thus making changes in a patriarchal system and they think that talking women out of their human rights will diminish their power in society.

Does any one of those men, and for certain women too, who are no different when in power know that if it was not for women that they would never be? It is time to end this and many other nonsense inequalities in this world. With the globalization there is no more room for this type of feudal mentality.

The planet is so interconnected nowadays that a health crisis in West Africa threats the whole West world with an Ebola outbreak. Funnily enough, as conveniently as the news about the outbreak in America about it suddenly vanished away.

The news of an Ebola outbreak threatening the world came to happen while they were fighting over racism issues regarding a policeman killing a disarmed black teenager, as big as to frighten the armed police officer; it completely disappeared after so many other menace of terrorism fabricated in the months that followed that terrible incident.

But although it turns out to be such a convenient and political weapon of mass distraction, we shouldn't think of the world as subdivided into categories, poorer countries, less advanced social and economic regions, a high society, a poor neighbor and less provided parts, underdeveloped world, etc, etc. Because, in the end, all peeled the layers of the onion, we as planet are one. If we continue to have that mentality of us against them, of fighting global poverty we will miss the train of thought that can take us to a more clear reality.

Nothing says more about inequality than poor and wealthy. But Happiness goes beyond economical crisis. It's an inner disposition that has nothing to do with social, economical, gender inequalities. And it has everything to do with an ulterior reason from an interior force, pulse, for being happy and helping others on finding their way to happiness. That's why I wrote the book "A-Z of Happiness". Finding your bliss in true equality and great quality can only benefit others, helping the world being more equal one step at a time.

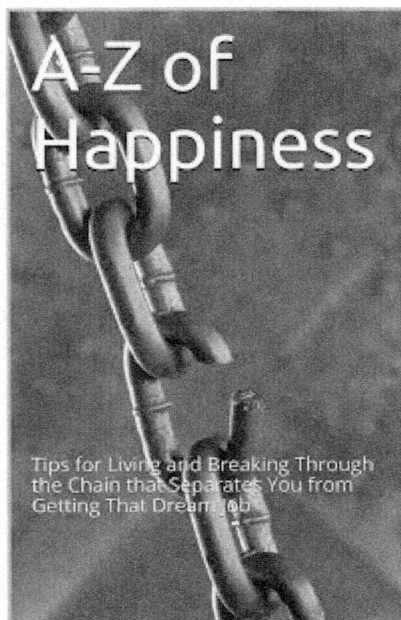

For example in Brazil, where inequality took such an unbalanced proportion that rich people live encapsulate in their own house and living side by side with slums, and the wealthy people have to be literally incarcerate inside their own mansion because they will risk being robbed or even worse, being assassinate if they put their feet outdoor.

The inequality became a knife with two points. And why inequality exists? In India, besides the economical plateau we still see the downturn in society.

There are also the religious issues. In Brazil the inequality has some similarities and although it is quite ambiguous it's clear that inequality comes from other things been too equal. That meaning in the other side of the scale there is a factor that distorts deeply this equation making it quite unbearable to see the facts. But the truth is while we fight to change these so controversial issues with the wheel spinning things that are in a very general and slight way improving.

Again in Brazil, poverty is decreasing and it's thanks to a political change in the way things were handled, not so much from a global political change but rather from private initiative that generated an avalanche of projects and perspective.

As a good result if in a continue process equals a better result in an exponential effect, the chances are that changes will happen in a happy merry-go-round way.

But we still see much inequality in places where issues such as Education and violence, health and home, transportation etc should already be resolved if we see that poverty is diminishing. But inequality still plays a major role because, let us face it: it's not making anybody less poor or people less rich than when or if we can wipe out inequality for good in the face of the earth. Vanished, gone... would that be a miracle, for sure!

We cannot and should not divide the world in rich and poor. Saying that violence against women are women issues also don´t help much either. That would actually only aggravate the problem. It´s everyone´s issues, for children to the elder, from

Asian to North America, from North to South. The problem here is not how many people or countries in this world have lack of education, home, a decent income, or whatever differentiates what's to live with dignity and what's to live with the dignifying amount of money.

It's the way we think of inequality that we need to change. It's not US versus, but much more UNI-versus, us together as one, no inequality means **no** to say that we may differ from others, we are no different than our neighbor, a country cannot differ from another if all of them lives on the same planet, breath from the same air, and depends on the same source. There is no inequality and period. Thinking like this sounds pretty silly, Utopian even.

There is no way to see inequality if we don't see it as nonexistent. Because if we ought to see reality as it is, inequality cannot be. Once we are all born equal and human rights are accessible to all and not only some, there will be no such thing as inequality.

What is the origin of misogyny, xenophobia and homophobia anyway? Why is there still so much violence against women, foreigners and homosexuals being perpetuated, and people thinking they have the right to do so much wrongs against the human rights?

Why is the female boasted to be so scary, menacing? And why the Amazons were considered legends instead of being defended and defined in the historical context as liberating and emancipating of the soul? If their tales and exploits were banned or punished, muffled by society and the power, but embedded in the human psyche and they survive until today.

The book that I recently published on Amazon covers the historical awareness of nature that both contributes to the perpetuation of inequality and the role of men and women in society in turn generating a distortion of power, values and principles that generate violence.

Dancing On Wor^I^ds

"Memoirs of an Amazon" is a story about past lives revealing mysteries and sliding over the realm of the imaginary that challenges mankind to the vision of a society free of prejudice to the eradication of the root of problems rather complex. And that vision would benefit both the arrival of a time of peace and the dissolution of discords and the solution of challenges between such misunderstandings that plagues the world today.

So talking about human rights, there are a lot of wrongs until we get it right as prejudice and contempt for citizens considered inferior, and any act of domination and discrimination on ethnic or national origin, including what is also considered a violation by the Conference United Nations Conference on Human Rights (Vienna, 1993), which formally recognized violence against women as a violation of Human Rights.

5

A Life Like Mine

"Where is Dawson when I most need him?"

She was only fifteen when she met Dawson. He was a handsome guy, going to high school, and she didn't have finished yet the elementary. She had to give up her studies to pursue a career, which her mother, an independent single-mother, had prepared to her.

Her grandmother was ill, dying from lung cancer, and her mother needed her, now more than ever, to help her in the factory, sewing the wedding dresses to her clients, who were extremely rich women, most of them married to politicians and other authorities who worked for the government. The wedding dresses were addressed to the daughters of modern aristocracy, which by the way, she assumed that she would be wearing one of those days.

Dawson had already asked her mother for her daughter's hand. Though her father was still alive, he disappeared from their lives since

Christie was nine years old. But Christie has just a few memories from her father's figure. His absence made her feel as if he didn't exist at all. He seemed to be more like a character of a poorly written novel in the mist of her own life than a dream that she had one day and she could not remember so well.

Her stepfather's disappearance coincided with her debut in a romantic relationship with herself, when she dreamed of a Prince Charming, culminating with the appearance of her best friend into her life. Art seemed to be the best guy to whom she could devote herself and she felt she could spend the rest of her life with him without hesitation or second thoughts. The problem was only that she also felt that she could have never met a guy like this in her life. And perhaps her perception was also right: A Cassandra's prediction that could ruin her entire dream of wedding him one day. Besides, he had too many troubles in his life to really pay attention to his friend's deepest feelings. Since she was a little girl, he kept being a major influence in her life. And although distant, he was still there for her, as he pictured himself on her eyes.

To explore her own soul there was not one person who could take care of her feelings better than her mother. Who knew her better than anyone else in this world?

Her mother was sweet and funny, and the "best mom" to translate into her own words.

Christie, as her own mother used to call her since she was born, attended the church every Sunday and prayed for her grandmother's soul.

But Art was her heart. He was the sweetheart to whom she would wed, and for him she would devote her life. She assumed she would marry him some day, as a passionate dream for which only a mature woman could wish. But she was still a girl; she didn't have the breakthrough that emphasizes the ability to make him being struck by her natural charm and her powerful talents.

Natural charm was her deed indeed. She was full of grace. Her walk was followed by a dance of a million stars. The sidewalk had a brilliant glimpse and no path would ever be the same again, after she passed over it.

She liked to laugh, and a lot. She seemed to be full of surprises, and her life was indeed an adventure in each corner of the risky highways that seemed to accompany her. Her personality was a mixture of passion and shimmering disdain. She could go from the angel who fell from the stars, with all her sympathy and respect, such a distinctive lady, to a nasty beast, or rather bitch who could devour a hundred wolves.

Her curled dark hair and her golden greenish eyes astonished the most glorious people used to deal with celebrities and neck breaking personalities in a daily basis. Was she an emerald hidden between rocks or the petals of an orchard in the middle of a bouquet of roses? She seemed to be blessed and her sincere nature surprised the most enlightened person. But what mostly impressed people by her beauty it was the intense light that was projected from her eyes.

Although her life was drifted by so many bad surprises, she seemed to surpass them with a graciousness that only an angel would encompass, as if she could fly away with white wings and a smile, and to all the right places.

Her skin was dark, yet it could even be considered very tanned by the sun, as she spent most of her time going to the beach and bathing on the ocean. And yet she almost never used to take a sunbath for the last few years after her friend died, and she felt so depressed that she did not go to the beach ever again.

In spite of it all her eyes had even more brightness by the contrast of her dark skin. Her father was French. Her mother was the most beautiful woman to whom he ever laid on his eyes. And she was born from a family who were slaves, and from a couple who got to being born free, being her grandfather a hard worker from the beginning of the century, who helped to build the highest buildings in New York City. His parents came from Africa, and the parents of his parents were slaves.

She looked so different from her mother that only her skin could explain that she came from an Afro-American family. At school, children would ask her if her mother had blue eyes, for her eyes being green, they wondered if any of her parents had blue or green eyes, and if her father had brown eyes, and her mother blue.

"My mother is an African-American woman, and I am too", she would proudly say. "And I have my mother's skin, and I came from her womb! I've got no father. I am born from a virgin mother..." she would answer to anyone who questioned her origins.

She would always state with every certainty in her bones that her mother was a virgin when she conceived little baby Christie, which was not totally incorrect. There held indeed some hidden truth on that. A mystery that maybe she was about to reveal. The guy who she met didn't know her deeply and didn't exactly succeed on his perpetrating intention.

He was afraid that someone would appear in the building where her mother worked as a sewer, and he did it before he could even reach her deeply.

He made her promise that she would shut up and do not tell anyone about what happened, to the risk of losing her job for she couldn't report a rape (he did have some letters from her saying that she loved him, enough evidence to get him rid of any judgment.) But she could put him on jail for sexual harassment. He was her boss after all.

So the very next day she called the police and made a complaint against him. He was put in jail for his sexual assault and this was but a heavy burden that he had imposed on her. And her daughter never wanted to meet "that bastard": that is how she called her own father.

70

Her mother worked hard to give her child the best that she could possibly provide for both of them. Her big brother was already in the run to a scholarship at Law Studies and he would soon be prepared to work as a lawyer. Jay was the best half-brother she could ever wish for. Although their differences were immense, with a gap from age to life style, there was a bridge that made the harmony for both of them as easily as happily as they could dare to encounter even between twin flames: both had a mother full of love for them and a smile full of sympathy and hopes.

Although her mother didn't give birth to her half-brother, she did treat him as if he came from her womb.

But they were the best violet purple love only soul mates could offer. Her half brother was generous to her, and now she lived in his apartment into an old building at the corner of Trenton Ave and York Street, in an obscure area of Philadelphia City.

He had been using the apartment that he bought five years ago, as an office for his law business affairs. But now he moved to New York, where he had many clients and he decided to close the apartment.

Christie wanted to use his apartment to give a big change in her life. She was tired of working at the factory with her mother and she decided that she wanted some independence. She was already nineteen and she thought that the accuracy of her life would support a life on her own.

Her mother was not at all satisfied with her "own made up mind" decision. After all "It's a big world out there..." as she told her daughter.

But then, what could she do with a girl so stubborn like that? She left her mother all preoccupied at her house in the Northwest of Washington DC.

. . . .

The next day, after she had moved from New York, the City that never sleeps, to D.C., THE City, and then back to Philadelphia, she goes to the shopping mall next to Juniper Street. The mall was empty since the September eleven attack. She came inside the Gap Store. There she bought a nice sweater that she had been enamored with for months, and a coat made of wool. She was about to meet a friend, Stephanie, also known as Fanny, which is the diminutive of Francis. And that is how she liked to be called. If she wanted to see a smile from her, she just had to treat her like a French royalty and call her Fanny. If she wanted to see her cracking out loud she would say her first name and her second with such a redundant result that would make the word "funny" sound silly to her, making it a funny world, after all.

Her sincerity and ability to make a fool of herself had her often taken as a clown between friends. And yet nothing could come further from the origin. Her royalty was expressed in each studied movement that she would make. Her name was given after Stephanie, the Princess from Monaco. Her own mother met the Princess of Monaco's mother, Grace Kelly, when she was still working as an actress in a studio in LA.

She was a former prodigious child star by then, but her career was over when her parents decided that it was time to move back to Paris, to an after-war France, for all the doors were open back then to return home. Since then, between tears of farewell, she promised her oldest fellow star, and companion of the same cinema's company, that she would give her child the same name as the actress. So she had four daughters; the oldest one was Grace, the second one, Kelly; then she came: Caroline. And her youngest daughter is Cristie's dear friend Stephanie Francis.

Her cousin, whose family stayed in America, just got married. And she knows that the best wedding dresses would come from her mother's hands. Besides, she was a major in fashion. So she was really used to understand the term "hot stuff" when it comes to the high fashion.

And she also knows where the name "haute couture" came from.

Once a man let her pass first on the bridge near her house. She hesitated, she didn't want to feel like she was a feminist, but she saw that he came first. She then noticed that he was just being a gentleman. But after a while the man got angry.

"They will do it on purpose... there are no more ladies in this world!" Another man, who had just seen the whole picture, would report to him that Stephanie was only playing a fool of him.

"Yeah, I can see that!" said the man, looking at the pretty doll who wore her hair in a French braid. Stephanie, a name which is also French, was French and, besides, Parisian and she was more than a lady. She felt herself like a Princess. But she was indeed a Goddess, with her cinematographic looks, with a face of an angel along with her sweet smile and her body to die for, and with her fashion that pretty much stayed a bit of obsessed with vintage clothes like in the forties. No, she was not in her forties, for she was even younger than Christie, although with her style she indeed looked much older. And she dressed like the movie star Laurel Bacall, someone she had been obsessed with since always, for her mother also knew that celebrity in person and had photos and posters of her in every corner of her house.

"Pardon me!!" she said with her strong and sexy French accent. "See, I am a foreigner and I don't know the rules here. S'il vous plait, vous pouvez m'expliquer ce que je dois faire en cette question la!"

Everybody looked at her as if she was an ET. And although sometimes she looked like an ET, with that entire old fashioned look mixed up with all her so modern way of living, beneath all that carcass and appearance that she projected to the outside world, she was a very humane, tender and caring person. She was such a character that could only exist in the Hollywood scene.

She wanted to get married soon, and she contacted Christie to get some information on how to make a nice treat for her wedding.

"I am so happy for her. I truly am. She met the right guy for her, and that makes her happy. And what makes my dearest sweet friend happy makes me happy too." Christie told to her mother. So there they met, at the shopping mall. From there they went to a Starbucks nearby.

"Christie, I was thinking...."

"No, really funny! Tell me, Fanny: you were thinking..."

"Yeah" she giggled, "What if I decide to marry in red? You know, despite the other's judgments. I want to look good... look good, you know!'

Christie could not pay attention to what she was saying after she used the word red. Red was her face then, and red was her passion for Art. Her heart was red and the color red seemed to follow her like a bloody trail. She could not take that girl's face out of her mind. Her head was full of a sanguinary tragedy, such an unpleasant memory that kept following her since she heard the news.

"What is going on, sweetie? You look pale..."

"I am sorry, Stephanie Fanny." She thought that perhaps her dearest of friends could help lift up her spirits. But even saying her name was sounding quite awkward then.

"I do not feel well lately. You may try to get an appointment with mommy. You just have to call her and explain to her what you want. I am not the best person you could get advices from today, darling. I need to go home now. I am sorry."

"Need a drive?"

"No, but thanks, anyway, dear. I can walk."

"Ok, so just keep walking..." And she laughed before she left for she knew that her last phrase was referring to the tale she had just confined to her about the incidental piece of work that was her former boyfriend Johnnie.

Then, I leave quickly. I go back to my brother's apartment and I get a message from the answer machine. The officer called me twice. He really needs to talk about the girl. Oh, man! What now? Do I really need to explain to them, again, and again, that I do not know that girl?

She takes a nap. During her sleep she hears a bell ringing again, with that celestial timber, as if a thousand angels touched it, as if announcing the end of a dreadful time and the return of the dead to their places. She wakes up, and looks at the watch before her: six o'clock; again, at the same time that she has been awakening each morning.

"Mom, how could you do that?? Not telling me about that? Keeping me away from the truth… Without thinking that one day I would finally find out about what happened that dreadful night where I was conceived?"

She couldn't believe her ears. The detective found much more out about her past than she could possibly know. She was not born from a "bastard" father as her mother had insinuating most of her life. In fact she wanted to have a baby with him and disappeared to the south in a faraway land of Brazil when she found out that she was pregnant. And it was there where she was born.

The man was not even convicted because the charges were dropped for lack of evidence. Later on, her mother came back to the States when she was only six years old. But Christie still remembered her childhood in Brazil like a treasure, or more like a dream.

"And you never told me that...Why? I always hated myself for being the product of a violent crime."

"I am so sorry, honey. It was the "mid-eighties". And women were so much for their liberation, to work hard and be independent, and to never allow a man to dictate them that it was more like a fashion to follow to be a single mother and take care of your own child."

"But then, all that you said about me not having a father it was all a lie to me... How could you do that to your own daughter?" Christie started to cry.

"Don't cry, sugar baby... I always wanted you all mine, and I couldn't conceive a man's figure in my life at that time. My father abused me when I was only two. And I hated men so much... And I was so afraid that this could happen again to my own child..."

She also starts to cry on the other line. She never thought that one day this would all go out, so easily like that, pouring directly from her soul to her eternal child. At least, that is what she supposed that she was doing. Because what she heard from the other side was a different cry. Christie had never heard her mother sigh so profoundly like that.

"What about me? Didn't you ever think that I would want to meet my own father someday?"

"But you hate the guts out of him..."

"Of course, mother! Who wouldn't? After all, telling such a story to a young innocent being?"

Meanwhile, Christie had the refrigerator open, as she was hungry for more information.

"Listen, Christie, little sugar! I do not want you to look for your father. I once was very much in love with him. And when I found out that he was cheating on me, and that I would have this child of mine. I realized it was too much to bear... Besides, he would turn just like your old grandpa, anyway! I know the type, believe me!"

"But I do have a father. And now I want to know him."

She doesn't respond.

Christie could not take this anymore. She hung up, after she saw a sweet apple pie looking at her and inviting her so voluptuously to insert her teeth on that red slice.

"Come, and eat me!" The pie would say.

She turned on the TV as she lied down over her bed. Too many lies and too many flies orbiting around, that even she was not certain to whom she would confine and what to believe anymore. And yet she could not quite grasp what was going on.

And she cannot stop the TV remote control, as it seems that she cannot even control her own life now.

She goes from one channel to another, to go channel surfing, making a rapper of a zapper, zapping like a zombie, without paying attention to no channel in particular. They all seem so filled with ads anyway. She feels herself being swallowed by a giant wave, from the aggressiveness of tasteless and endless TV commercials, between senseless images and nonsensical (and not at all lyrical) jingles.

A dog that bites its owner... and there was another dog who talks. And now came two cats complaining with another lazy cat, about their smelly 'pots'. What about the cats singing a chorus: what are they really selling, by the way? Was that Cats, the amusing musical on TV??

There it comes another senseless one: it was about a boy who, having a hard time cleaning his greasy hands, throws away sweaty and bloody-tomato sauce filled with the hamburger that can kill you from high cholesterol. Then it comes another ad (that adds nothing else, but pure tasteless images) of that jelly that you better spill it out, or you will get diabetes just by watching it. She leaves the CNN channel on, live while she's still alive.

"A wave of accusations of satanic cult and child abuse is been investigated. Religious believe that this might lead to an inquiry into this growing fascination with dark cults and with diabolic forces." The reporter says. She puts the volume high up.

"Some say that the cults are somehow related to the latest terrorist attacks in NYC and also have connections with the culture of cocaine at the former coffee plantations in Colombia.

A series of allegations have been presented and a murder of a twenty-three year old woman has been treated as an unjustified case. FBI officers say..."

She turns off the TV. She knows what the FBI says about it.

6

CYBER ATTACKS

Sony Pictures allegedly says that it recently suffered a cyber attack by North Korea which made it withdraw the film *The Interview* which is about an assassination plot against the North Korean president Kim Jong Un, and banning it from the theaters. The American President Barack Obama declared that Sony shouldn't bow and be taken down from such threat. And he did it right. If I was the President of the United States I would do the same. You shouldn't convey to a foreigner's demand, when it's related to terminate what's on the Constitution, the right (and duty) of having freedom of speech. And the Arts Entertainment Industry should be the last one to have been suffering from such retaliation. So what? Sony declares that it was the North Korean Government that made a threat that they would bomb the theater, i.e. because of the terrorist attacks in the theaters if and only if they would dare to show up with that movie. And then Sony resumes the case saying that they are studying the matters carefully, and that they shall release only the film only in the internet channel.

Ok. I'm not an insider and I don't work for Sony Pictures so I don't have any juicy gossip or can I spill the oil for them. Fortunately, or unfortunately, and I cannot do it. So I am not a good material to rely upon when dealing with internal affairs. But I know about publicity. Being in the market for quite a while to see so many hoaxes and things made believe to go and believe in them right away. So, that studying the matters carefully, if my guess is right and it's quite often so, I understand as saying they are investigating which marketing strategy is the best for that kind of movie. Who is going to see a comedy about North Korea? Only nerds, right? Nerds go to the movie theater. Yes, they do. They will go watch a movie that they would most be related to their consumerism. They are not going to pay for a movie that's "garbish", a mix of garbage and gibberish. That they will get from the internet anyway. They are in their comfortable seat, sitting in front of a computer and that's... in a click, the film is down-loadable in a second. "SO", Sony thought, "why bother taking the time and spending money with that?" So, Sony knows about that. They do have their researchers. They pay a lot of money for them, to have a glimpse of what's going on in the minds of the audience and movie goers alike.

So, now, if you were a Producer, and you are having financial problems, you are big like a Goliath loosing against a small chain. And the last couple of movies didn't quite give back as much as you expected and you sworn that is losing the battle against the swords of piracy. And you even lack the time and money to spend in excessive publicity, so what would you do? Exactly!

And I'm not saying that they are wrong here, as I don't play along and I like a more impartial view, with no strong opinions, I'm no biased based. I just give my two peanuts, as I do not have any pennies... I'm a woman with my own convictions. And I know nothing is written in stones. Not even when it's written in a tomb.

They did what any clever publicist would do anyway and they took the matters in their hands, they didn't play the victims of the circumstances and... game on! They forced a situation under threat. After all, I learned a long while ago that any publicity is good publicity.

I'm not implying here that they fabricated the threat. I'm far from that supposition even if the US government didn't give credits to the terrorist threats in the first place. Secondly, they changed the argument so very disturbing as it was.

The threat may quite be as real as the hair of the North Korean President. What I am saying here is that their suffering so many cyber attacks, having the leakage of their files, and hackers getting in their hairs, and going through their emails making them available for all to take a look and getting their scripts and even before a film has been released, they then decide it was time to take <u>advantage</u> of the situation. I say, advantage, not advance.

Even the new movie of the famous British agent James Bond that's about to be released in the end of this year (2015) had the first draft, or an early version of its script, *Spectre*, stolen. So now, you are threatening the famous spy and you don't think you are going to get burned? That's what happens when you mess up with Bond... James Bond. Watch out, you criminals... MGM and family members will go after anyone who steals or uses the script for its own profit, to sell it elsewhere. And they are so damn right, they own Bond films rights, for Bond's sake! But then again, if you know the end of the story, and you happen to read the script before you even think that film existed, would that stop you to go to the movie theater?

Of course, you know the end of the story... Bond will win in the end. Unless they want some other actor to replace Daniel Craig for a new British goodie, there you will have it: The 007 agent always win against the bad guys in all his action movies. So there you had it. Sorry, I did not flash the spoiler alert here... Now, you see, who's going to watch that movie after knowing who is going to win in the end? Just like everyone, and everybody else, and if you are a fan of Bond's movie like I am, you will even watch it twice. So, what is the big deal about having their data stolen if that won't crash their system, and instead it would even instigate people to go watch their movies? Exactly!

It's for sure a good free publicity for their movies, something they have been breaking their bones about, burning their brains out, and blowing their minds up when they know that YOU CAN TAKE ADVANTAGE OF cyber attacks and make them work in your favor. That meaning, they take action in a marketing move. And if you can do that so they can. And yes, they can!

And then I said advantage, not advance, and you know why? Because if they thought in advance, they had already made a movie about hacking and having Bond investigating the case of stolen scripts! Now, that's a good plot. And that would be a god damned marketing movie, I mean, move. And there you have people asking: James Bond has a script?

And don't let me start with the crying game. Moneyhorse game has already capitalized in a good kick-start of its *Glorious Leader!* As they took advantage of the "out-of-hand" situation and they put Obama as the pilot and his hand on the wheel to make a game as topical as possible including Barack Obama in the leadership, and no dealership, piloting a TIE fighter. Game on!

And who would wonder? They had already planned to launch the game over the internet and asked permission to Sony and Microsoft (although the latter rejected the pact), more like a disturbing distribution package deal, BEFORE the cyber attacks... hmm, hmm. Ok, then, all so well planned. So that's a marketing plan. Maybe after a good first market-selling Microsoft will be a majorly soften up its standard and accept to play the game.

And if you are still sorry for Sony Pictures saying, "What if that had happened to you, that someone would steal your stuff, go through your computer, check out your emails, etc, etc, wouldn't you be mad too?"

First of all, an invader did indeed go through my stuff, when they broke into my house and took all my personal belongings, including my computer, an i-pod and a video camera (yes, at that time I still used a camera that needed a small video tape). And that's where I had all my files, including all of books documents and my pictures and images that I didn't have saved anywhere else. So now you have it.

But then again you may say, "But you are not big enough to complain, you didn't miss much." Yes, it's true. At that time I was not even a bestseller as I am now becoming.

Someone recently bought my Historical Fiction *Amazons from Ancient to Medieval Times* in England, the one I wrote in Portuguese and I instantly became a bestselling novelist for my book reached number one in the kindle store. And there again, now in Spain, for someone just bought my book *Pierrot & Columbine* in Portuguese and all of a sudden I'm number four on sales over foreign fiction in the Mystery/Suspense genre or "Policiaca Negra y Suspense". Olé! Ok, I won't make such a fuzz out of it... it's already too hairy. I should have meant a fuss, I know. Besides that's no biggie.

So, how about Brazilian President Dilma's emails and phone calls being monitored and intercepted by the NSA, as Edward Snowden, ex-CIA employee who became number one enemy of America's government after declaring that and many other top secret surveillance the American agency did. And they did not only do it to her, but also Angela Merkel and Vladimir Putin were their targets, with many other international secrets revealed by the wiki leaks files? Because they are not there to spy in their private lives. They are there for political and economic advantages.

No wonder now Petrobras is under the scrutiny of the public view, once they find out a big scheme of corruption going on underneath the Brazilian enterprise's eyes when they bought Pasadena for an overpaid price. So now if it isn't a mischief, that's the ruin of any country... And if you go back yet, you will find out that America had always that hidden agenda of damaging and put South America on its knees, to subdue the whole region and its people in the most manipulative way.

Dictatorship in South America is no big secret, as they are not top secrets anymore all the torture they made on people who went "astray", that meaning not according to their purpose and big scheme or plan, and the US had a big hand on it all helping the military actions in Chile, Argentina and in Brazil, oh well, most countries and that's no coincidental that it's also there where most Nazis went to flee, yet not be free of its accusations. So now, that's big stuff. And if YOU think you are free from all that stuff, think again, the "implants" are everywhere, from internet connections to individual computers AROUND THE WORLD. "Private eyes, they are watching you... watching your every move... Oh yes!"

In 1940, when Charles Chaplin, the founder of United Artists before it became MGM's, made the movie "*The Great Dictator*" America was still at peace with Germany. And they depicted a satirical, ridiculous, dumb figure out of who would later become an international threat and the most tyrannical and voracious killer in the world's history. And the movie was the most successful finally speaking to the industry at that time. It warned people about the threat? Yes. But it gave bunches and bunches to their pockets in turn. All was planned to give them their financial gain.

And now some theaters decided to play *The Interview*, that pretty stupid comedy about the plot for the assassination of the North Korean dictator. And it's when? Exactly, right at Christmas time, a bad taste movie for a big dumb audience who doesn't know any better than buying popcorn and sit their big assets over the chair to go watching a terrible movie. And no, I didn't watch it and I don't even have to, just by learning about the plot and having a second of the trailer been thrown out in my face by News stations, I do not even need a second guess.

So if this isn't a big plan to get people to the movies, I don't know what else is. I said some theaters, because they all knew in first hand that this film wouldn't get people's attention if not by some political strategy. Because theaters would lose money if they all showed up with a movie that wouldn't return its budget, they were closing down on it. But once they got media's attention by fabricating and manipulating the masses (and that is all over the world) then they had one or two doors open for them to show their movie. They learned well, as much as Hitler did about propaganda.

And that's also to show that North Korea had a plan to attack the States: by a weapon of mass distraction. Or rather by China's unicorn, I mean Unicom (a state-owned telecommunications company that runs not only China but its neighbor as well). China control's over North Korean computers shut down their internet for over two days in a row and a day before Christmas (that meaning the end of year 2014), showing that they were actually pretty powerless over their claims of being able to have a cyber attack, although they have declared not guilty over the whole ordeal.

But to see that the counterespionage came from random parts of the globe, using servers such as in Bolivia, Thailand and Singapore just display the incapacity of all the espionage task to spy on each other, as the breach among them is so vast and it's getting even more widespread. It's like a cancer, difficult to battle because of its own camouflage does not allow it to be seen and its nature is to hide among many other good cells. So how come they find out of such acts of cyber attacks?

Files from Snowden were revealed on the German magazine *der Spiegel* showing that the NSA had already hacked the North Korea by installing malware in their computers in early 2010.

The point here is how they attacked Sony. Because if the NSA was planting backdoor malfunction in their system, how come would they be able to attack them in turn? Did North Korea really hack the heck out of it? To lay such a question on the table is like asking, "Which came first, the chicken or the egg?" That leaves a question hanging like crickets into a dark night: "Why would the US Government allow this attack after all?"

The hackers did indeed manipulate media to embarrass Sony, or was Sony solely in a direct way involved on that, or their former sour ex-employees who got fired, and fired them back up. Would they all have been so skillfully manipulative to get the news coverage in the hands of strategically-chosen channels and reporters so that it would have the free marketing campaign for such a bad movie, that couldn't do the job by itself the whole time through? Plus it solves the problem on how to spread their power and have even more control over the internet, thus planning in advance to manipulate masses with access to the web?

"Look what we discovered until now about this girl: she was a Colombian student with an irregular Visa that had been expired for six months," said Jay to Gail.

Christie decided to go get some sleep, while they both talked on the dining room. She heard the door slam. Jay left, and Gail tried to fit on the small sofa. She was shivering, enrolled on her leather coat.

Christie then got some covers for her. Now she could say that she was indeed an "under cover" agent.

"I met him. He had heroin inside his leather coat's pocket. We took him to the police department. You can see him if you want to. Go give him a visit at the prison," said Gail with a monotone voice.

Christie cried once again. So, indeed he was really there. And she was a victim that he tried to persuade to be infected by his dirty hands.

"Why didn't he ever tell me that?"

She called the detective the next day, that handsome man who saved her: That semi-god who seemed as interested on her as a blank paper in a mind of a writer in the middle of a block crisis. She said… well, she had nothing to say, which sounded even more pathetic on the phone. Such a terrible indulgence that she had got herself into and that would explain her nails been beaten and that had her scratching her skin in a furious act. That was just a little bit too much for her to stand. She sipped and she slipped onto the rug and tried to sleep. She sobbed and sorted a piece of paper over her hand and she cried. She stopped before she grabbed the phone and whispered some nonsensical monosyllabic words.

"Han, detective?" There were only crickets sounding over the line. And that was what she was most afraid of if or when she called him. There was no answer.

"Are you there on the other line?" she insisted as stubborn as she used to be to everything that defied her senses.

"Yes. Hello there, ma'am. What do you need?"

Oh, what do I need? I am going to tell you what I do need.

"So... You caught him. You have your guy now. So…"

"Yep. What can I do for you?"

"I just wanted to hear your voice…that's all!"

She just wanted to hear his voice?

"Come on! Didn't you have anything more important to say? Or at least avoid the embarrassment and be more realistic? Come on, you are blowing everything up now!" she thought to herself.

"Do you want me to hang up so that you could get the answer machine?" He patiently waited in the other line.

"It is just that…"

"Yes?"

"I could not stop thinking of you…"

"Now I sound even more ridiculous, like a pop music being played in a disco in the middle of the 80's."

She sounded terribly sorry, like a intermittent purple neon light coming from the window. Just like the video clips from her mother's recollection that she sneaked at one afternoon when she had nothing better to do.

There where everybody is too drunk, or too deaf from the high pitch that plays non-stopping, to really care about the lyrics that comes out of a soft voice anyway…

"…Since the day that I met you."

There! She just ruined everything up, right at the tip of her tongue through the top of her lungs.

"Well, I do not have the drug to cure that. I do not have a solution for that!"

"Ha, Ha, ha!" She laughed out loud. Totally brushy all blush blustered and busted. She just screwed the whole thing up in less than two minutes for being really crazy over the entire issue. She just laughed and laughed.

"At least it is a happy nervous laughter!" he wittily noticed.

She laughed even louder. Though she never touched any drug in her entire life (well, at least not from her free will, there was that time when some guys offered her a drink and it turned out to be the date rape drug). And now she was totally in ecstasy just a couple of minutes ago, and then she had become a piece of garbage, just ready to be thrown away.

"I stink!" she said to herself.

"You sound like a school girl!"

"Ha, ha, ha! Look at what I became."

"What?" he laughed back at her.

"A schoolgirl?"

"Oh, man!" Now he had really thrown her right from the higher level of the tallest skyline, right at the top of the highest building of New York City, a title which is now back to the Empire State.

She had just felt like being crashed and smashed her skull right there on the sidewalk. And here it came, another word and she felt like a truck had split her up into two pitiful pieces of shit.

"I weep as I whip myself up." She thought; then she calmed down.

"Yeah, yeah, I am like a child right now. What can I do to get this ecstasy out of my body? Bad girl!"

"Shame on you!"

That is still she saying all that to herself, and beating her up, just to shake her out of her shame and back to her senses.

"But since you got my man, I became a child eager to be taught how to live again all by myself."

"I'm so sorry!" she said instead. "I do not know what is happening with me." She said so, sobbing a little, and then weeping like a crow. And she continued to drag.

"I think that I am just too stressed out and I needed to talk to someone. I am so ashamed. I am so sorry!"

Oh, did she say the forbidden word for all métiers: "Sorry?"

Since she had watched the movie *Love Story* she had put into practice that special advice that Ryan O'Neil, playing that mixed of sweet/sour character Brian, gave to his father.

"To love is to never say I am sorry!" Well, he didn't say that. But at least that is what she heard from her heart. He whispered over the phone instead.

"I do remember you like coffee. So why don't you come over one day and we have a nice cup of coffee."

"Cup of coffee sounds great. Besides you owe me that a long time ago. I am still waiting and the coffee is getting cold."

"Maybe coffee doesn't sound like a crazy idea, after all. Maybe this way I can wake up from this bad dream and smell the coffee."

Later that day, Christie went to the prison. There where he lied, her once loved now hated, now loved again Dawson. There he sadly waits for her. She looked at him, and he looked so pale.

He didn't say much. She kept questioning him about the whole stuff. He pretends he cannot hear her.

She quit. When she was about to leave, he calls her, softly.

"Christie," he says. "Would come over here for a sec? I'd like to say something."

"Oh, finally!" she said.

"Just one thing…" he touches her ear and spread his three most favorite words that he used to tell her every time she looked mad. And that would be the very last time that it would come out of his mouth and that she had just read inside his head: "I love you!"

She slapped his face. He looks at her even more perplexed.

"How dare you say that you love me? Do you know how much I have been suffering all these months?"

"I'm so sorry! I didn't mean to hurt you. I didn't say anything to spare you of suffering, and look what happened?" He starts to cry.

She grabbed his head, looked deep inside his beautiful deep dark eyes, and she looked at him as if he was not made of flesh and blood, as if he was only a spectrum of that man who she once knew.

"That is okay!" she said, almost whispering. "I will try to get you out of here. I don't know. I am going to call my brother, and see what he can do about that."

He stopped crying and he dried his tears with the tip of his sleeves.

"I just have one more question to you, and I promise I will leave…" She turned her back, as she dried a tear or two coming down her eyes, and she faced back at him. She completely tried to disguise her own exasperation.

"What exactly happened that night? What about the girl?"

"She was a girl from Colombia. I didn't know her. She was there to bring more drugs to the people there…"

"And the guy you kissed, you said, darn, draw, or you meant Daw? Was that a boyfriend of yours that I didn't know?

"You seem more like a Pandora's Box full of astounding surprises: the more we shake it the more we take it."

"Which boy?"

"The boy who kissed me and then you kissed him... I was high, but I saw the whole thing... I mean, scene, didn't you know that?"

"Oh, man! You might have misunderstood...He was no boyfriend, sweetie. He was just a man there I was trying to save..."

Well, at least that is what she wanted him to believe. Oh rather that's what she was trying to make him believe first and foremost.

"He was having troubles as he was unable to breath. I think he got too much smoke in his lungs. And then, I was there trying to make mouth-to-mouth breathing... See, baby, you've got that all wrong!"

"And it seems that another guy, who later I found out, was an undercover agent was doing exactly the same first aid procedure on you."

"All right, then. I will call my half-bro and see what he can do about that, ok?"

"Thanks, sweetie!"

She was leaving the room but before that she turned her back to take a last look at him; he pointed at his heart, and said in a wordless way like he always did to her.

"You will be always in my heart"

Two days have passed since she visited Dawson into prison. She couldn't get any sleep ever since. She went to the drugstore to get some aspirins. As she drove back home she found a place at the Walnut Street where there was written in neon lights: "Psychic READINGS for five dollars".

She definitely needed that right now. Five dollars, to pay the meter... But then she remembered that she had some coins left in her purse, so she decided to give it a try and get a reading.

"Who knows what I could find out about this case..." she said to herself.

A woman in her early fifties and a red turban on her head came to her aid with a smile that showed all her teeth made of gold.

"May I help you?" She finally said revealing a chain worth a million dollars.

"I hope so!" She said

She looked at her as if she had seen her before.

"Yes, I know. It is about your boyfriend and that night when you saw that black cat."

"What?" she asked.

"Yeah, I know everything about it. Don't need to tell me. It is already here" and she touched Christie in her forehead. "It is written right there in your mind. Girl, you've got some issues in your heart too. Let me see your hand."

She extended her arm and let her hand being open by the gypsy lady who stared at her with hypnotic eyes. She let her read her palm. But instead the woman just looked at her eyes. And she did that with no hesitation.

"I see a black cloud in your eyes, like a hole of a dark tunnel."

Christie had a smirk; she couldn't bear being so bare in front of that woman who tried to strip her off like a banana. And she took a step back.

"Anything that is not lived becomes to you like a devil." She spells out like a curse.

She took her hand off of her reach. Christie shook he whole body nervously.

"I don't know. Maybe I came to the wrong place. I am not so sure about that. I think it was not a good idea to come here after all...sorry! Good-bye!" And she went her way to the door to leave as fast as she could.

She looked outside the window. The leaves of the fall ran with the wind, and a twister was created with the circle of a stone, or more like a rock, dancing in the middle of the streets.

The sun embraced the sidewalks in a calm and lucid kiss.

Christie was about to leave when the woman stopped her.

"Wait!"

"What?" Christie took her hand off the door handle.

The gypsy pointed her index finger which seemed to have an implanted red nail, so big it looked like a huge stream of blood right at her heart; she did touch Christie's blouse, even after she had turned back to the door.

"I'm going to give you a tip and this will be for free: Take a nice look at your heart, and then you can find the answer."

"It is in there that all the answers that you've been so eagerly seeking can be found."

"Oh, man! I really have to get going. This was not indeed the right place. What a fiasco that this all have been. She's so fake! This woman knows no tiny thing... "

"Before you leave, just know that there is no wrong place to go. They are always right in the time that they are supposed to happen."

Christie gets into her car that she had parked just beside the shop where she left Stephanie. She had gone to her friend's house and she drove to the detective's office. She really needed some things to be explained to her. And there was no psychic who could let the words out for her. She didn't get it all, why it all happens the way they do, with no clues about the whole situation that seemed unbearable now more than ever.

Then she decided to ask the detective some questions now. She was tired of just having to give him answers. It was her turn to inquiry. She felt definitely going in the right path, as she had decided that it was time for him to reveal himself and answer her about things that has been bothering her. And she needed to clear things out.

On the way to the office, a black cat crossed the street just in front of her. It looked directly at her eyes, like saying, "I do know you, I met you before." Then, it ran as if it was scared by something.

She went for the meeting with the detective. She started to ask him questions, about the girl, and especially about her boyfriend.

"Don't you know? Nobody informed you?" He asked her, after all her talking and no responses.

She had her heart bouncing from one side to the other. The day was already full of surprises for her. The sun was hot, unusual for the end of November, and the blue sky melted with the white clouds.

"A coffee-shop hacker used a side-channel signal to attack computers. And researchers found the strongest signals came from computers operations that had their processors access off-chip memory."

"Could you put it in blunt English, please?" she said.

"Your computer was hacked…"

"How come?" Her heart was pounding out of her chest.

"The criminals, who they later found out were teenagers, broke into the Department of Defense and used your data to crash into the military organizations. They had stolen Top Secret US government files."

7

SPIRITUAL ALZHEIMER

Robin Williams' interview with David Letterman at the Late Show on November 30, 2009 about Rio winning as the 2014 City Host of the World Cup over Chicago created a fuss, at least in Rio. The comments were terrible indeed. After all "50 strippers and a pound of blow" to compete with Michelle Obama and Oprah wouldn't buy a thing, and wouldn't do FIFA any good, not even give a laugh out of it. But it surely enough cost him his life! He became so depressed of having to apologize about it and his apologetic words didn't have any effect after all.

Some strange coincidences in Robin Williams death though. His death on August 11, 2014 in a full moon had people perplexed. Two days later, day 13 and the candidate for the Presidential Elections in Brazil, Eduardo Campos died on a plane crash, at 13:13 (i.e. one pm and thirteen minutes; in Brazil we use to count time in a round until 23:59 to then go back to zero). Again some considered it a well planned plane "Accident".

The British BBC3 channel was shocked when they heard about Williams' death since they had just aired an episode of the American adult animated sitcom *Family Guy* showing him in many facets, and then in the end he is so overwhelmed by all his

SPIRITUAL ALZHEIMER

personae that he tried to kill himself.

In the movie *What Dreams May Come* where the character who played his wife had committed suicide he goes to the doors of hell to go try finding her. Then when he did die he encounters his heavenly friend saying to him, "what's the point of living until you are sixty "free" for eternity".

He died at sixty-three.

No wonder he was a controlled man. In the movie *Bicentennial Man* he was a robot, in *Hook* off the hook he was *Peter Pan,* a man who didn't want to grow up, and in *Aladdin* he was a slave genius, but then there he finally got his freedom, although he was so happy that he didn't know what to do with it at first.

A cartoon showing him as many characters, manipulating him to the bones, blowing his mind up, all that sounds like a creepy satirical way of making someone want to dig a hole and bury himself on it. But more manipulating than that it was to make a whole story happening before it did actually happen and showing it off in our faces.

There is an episode from *The Simpsons* which aired where they predicted that Germany would win the World Cup in Brazil, after Homer Simpson as the judge of the last game didn't comply with the organized crime that tried to manipulate him into making Brazil win. So it was still March when they aired it saying that Germany would become the champion over Brazil, overshadowing so many years of glory for Brazilian craziness for soccer. And then they depicted the whole cheerful spectators in Brazil.

"They never saw Brazilians so depressed!" the narrator says.

So if that's not mind blowing, that's no coincidence. It's just to show how much a manipulative scheme is made simply to demoralize an entire nation. And sure they did. If you notice the frowned face President Dilma Rousseff made while near German Chancellor Angela Merkel who in turn had a big smile over her face before the game was on and won, you would know what I mean. Dilma already knew that the game was lost. And that was even before it had begun. That's called match manipulation in favor of a marketing plan.

A big scheme was made and ADIDAS was the target. It was just so that the brand would be engraved in our brains while we watched the whole thing.

There is a corruption going on a global scale. But then again, some can even blame the Indians (the Germans chose to stay with the Natives from the Pataxo tribe, in an isolated patch in Bahia). And one can only guess that was due to the place and its magical effect, and the Indians giving herbs to the German team so that they would be so powerful to win the World Cup. And sure indeed they were incredible... Bravos!

And there is so much more in this than meets the eyes. The only one place where you are as safe as hell (or Nirvana) is in your third eye, or while you can be in a deep sleep.

But even in your dreams you may be manipulated by all things mundane, from the external excitements, as it may well show up for you.

If you dream of a train crash and you have seen a movie about it some days earlier, then your mind has been manipulated. But if you happen to dream of a kidnap (which I did a couple of days ago) and you wake up and watch in the news the very same morning that we were in this nightmare and at the same time that when you were dreaming about the kidnapping there was really happening a kidnap in your own city, so close to you, you may not have been dreaming that after all, but this could easily be a case of a lucid dream or you were having an astral projection.

But then if you dream of a plane crash and that happens some days later, this might well be a premonition. Thus to be certain the only place where you may well be one hundred percent sure you are who you are with no influence from other parties whatsoever is in your third eye. The inner eye in your brow works as a self God and it sees everything, that's the only safe realm where no one can touch your mind, but you.

Movies are made to be mind controlling. Movies created as dreams such as George Melies did, the first and maybe the only one who made it his own illusion to become a way of freedom

SPIRITUAL ALZHEIMER

from mind controlling.

The knowledge of Hitler's use of propaganda to manipulate, mobilize and elate the masses is wide spread. And he also used movies to create a mass emotion, commotion and devotion from people. And so did America in the awakening of the Industrial civilization.

Facebook studies of behavior reached to the point of having them declaring that they did manipulate information; they messed up with their data and omit others in people profile's timelines just to see what would be their reactions towards good and bad news.

Facebook manipulates masses. Period.
FIFA manipulated masses. Period.

They are all weapons of mass distraction. But if you see in another point of view they pretty much signify a lack of judgment from our parts. Because honestly thinking in a clear way we are the ones who can control what we see and what we do, and if you are willing to be manipulated so easily like this that should be your problem. The problem is that now there are even some conspiracy theorists (or terrorists?) saying that they are putting Fluoride in our water supplies because Fluoride is supposed to debilitate the pineal gland, the one located in our third eye and responsible for a spiritual response. They supposedly shut down any possibility for our spiritual awakening. And by them, I mean, who specifically? Have we been all drinking too much fluoride that scientists say it's good for your teeth but in the end that's all planned to kill any evolutionary state in order for us to keep being dumb? What we should fight against is a virus that spreads too rapidly. And I'm not talking about Ebola in Africa or the avian flu that's back in China and had already menaced the West. It's "the virus of stupidity" just to quote David Letterman in his recent program where he was showing some videos to the style of America's Funniest Home Videos reality TV programs. Those are the

Weapons of Self-Destruction.

Back on quoting the super fantastic comedian Robin Williams in his movies, a <u>Goodreads group</u> made me think of a movie not yet been mentioned there, <u>The Final Cut</u>. As I stated there, I know it was not his best film, and it features not his best asset which is his comic way, when he plays the best characters.

But I guess he couldn't help portray a bit of a dark humor in a particular saying, that makes now people who are fans of the movie and the actor wonder if it was in the script or if he added that line (like a deadline) with a bit of pepper.

The quote that I'm talking about in that movie is when he was at the library playing his character as Alan Hakman and he asks, "Is suicide under Self-Help?"

This simple line depicts so realistically what was really happening inside his head. It was too prophetical, too real, or rather surreal, and way too close, or "a little too close" to quote the merchant from Aladdin, and I can still hear his voice saying that in my head...

Now that I'm reediting and translating my books from <u>The Memoirs of An Amazon</u> Series, <u>Amazons from Ancient to Medieval Times</u>, <u>Amazons in Medieval Europe</u> and *Amazons Today* (soon to be released), almost in the same way as an editor would transplant memories in that film, it makes me think where the memory implants are located so that it would record so many past lives. Is that in the pineal gland, also known as the seat of the soul or the gateway to enlightenment (i..e., mind the gap between your eyebrow to put light in the mind's eye)?

Such a powerful structure the size of a pea, mirrored exactly in the same way in the left and the right hemisphere of the brain, could this really be the key to our origins and the source of all the stars stuff of which we were made?

This gland is also known for the *psychic* activities and paranormal abilities and it serves well as a third eye. It can also trigger vulnerability and it is often related to matters of chemical imbalance in our brains which in turn can lead to depression. Once said that, it is not hard to believe that suicide attempt is

SPIRITUAL ALZHEIMER

associated with a form of self-help process.

And it was not long ago that a young woman suffering from a terminal brain cancer took her life (and got the right to do it so) because of her unbearable crisis, which she had to dwell with painful headaches. I'm not a psychiatrist and in no way I'm devoted to any suicidal thoughts or pro-suicidal programs. I'm just so further from that in fact that I am totally pro-survival. And that's why I am quite sure that Robin Williams cut, I mean quote in that movie was more like a cry for help. And since he got no help from the outside world he had to rely on him, in an inner strength to battle his own crisis.

How many Williams are now suffering alone, even going through rehab programs and yet not recovering from terrible losses, unable to helping themselves or being helped?

In my book **Dearer Mirror** I expose the necessity we all have to self-knowledge to dive into our own selves so that we may emerge from this dumbness that makes us all sometimes believe we were less than what we potentially can become. And we laid on lies that make us mirror ourselves in illusions told to us as the truth and dismissing what is true as we thought were myths and legends, missing our life purpose and a real chance to spiritual awakening our superpowers.

I so wish that I could help as many people out there with my books not classified as self-help genre, but which they are in a way. So keep an eye for within the next couple of days or so I will let this and many other "Self Help" books available on the shelves.

If you know anyone undergoing any type (and I mean, ANY) of dismissing or self-destructive behavior, be an angel, say a word or two, and pass on my writings so that they will know that they too belong to something greater that the obscurity they feel now are nothing but clouds passing by; be true, be love, be light, be alive in de-light!

It does not bother me to have my writings being criticized in a bad light, although sometimes they are way too painful to watch how people have their minds so manipulated that they do not recognize good literary works.

And that´s just so because they are already too addicted, if not conditioned to believe in stuff that they wouldn´t otherwise if they were not entangled in that system. But what puzzles me most is when people read me and yet don´t get it, don´t have even a grasp of what I´m saying and cannot even go through the first chapter.

And again they expect something and it´s not anything to do with what they expected. Of course not, if these are my original thoughts and ideas, how come would you have read that in any other place? Unless piracy came on the way and some weirdoes took my publications and publish my books elsewhere and copied me, my books are one of a kind.

So it is not my fault that they´ve got lazy brains that they cannot think for themselves and get into their own conclusions. If they came to my book it was for a good reason. There must have been a hidden message for them somewhere there in between the lines. It´s my job to display them and express them in the best possible way but it´s still their job to go find the messages hidden between the lines. Get it? I know you do, you have already passed the test AND the first few chapters here from this book.

In the last two months I've already translated more than five books from other writers and if you add mine on that count the numbers will double with no doubt in the double of the double of it. They are all books that explain a methodology, except for the ones I just published which are novels.

I also write books with my own techniques and methodology. They usually do very well, better than my novels, for sure! One specifically good to awaken some psychic powers is <u>The DAO Workbook Illustrated</u>.

Some of my workbooks were recently purchased but one reader made me wonder what makes one person buy a book by mistake. If this person gives me a bad review because of his own fault, of not paying attention to what's inside, i. e. the technique of the content, you cannot blame the author or the book, and by that I say that I´m not the least responsible for that mistake. The

SPIRITUAL ALZHEIMER

reviewer so knew that that he even wrote it was his own fault.

I'm talking about my book <u>How to Make a Book</u> from my series *How-To* or, more specifically, <u>Como fazer um Livro</u> and the series in Portuguese is called *Como fazer com lazer*.

Funny enough it was my Portuguese version that had people (well for me one person is people enough) confused (and in my own mother tongue!) Of course it was in Portuguese, but even then it's not that confusing if I explain in the description of the book that it's a handmade material. The review I got from this person made me only smile: I was not wrong and yet I got a bad evaluation.

Things are not really fair in the publishing market, if they were all right I would be a bestseller and Dan Brown oh, well, he would be selling "do-nuts". Just kidding. To me, he could well be selling tickets to the Louvre, which he surely did, in an indirect way, anyway (Where is he now, by the way? I am missing all that fuss about Leonardo da Vinci).

So who knows one day I will become a bestseller and then I will have nothing else to complain about, ha-ha! But don't worry; until that day arrives I will be fighting like <u>Cats and Squirrels: The Amusing Quarrel</u> *(another workbook I wrote)*.

If you are anything like me and love to learn something new, even by mistake, and wish to know more about Arts & crafts, my books can just be that fix you need, even if 'by mistake' as I don't believe in things happening by accident. They surely are a good therapy practice, if you take the matters to your own hands.

And for all sake, have fun in <u>cool-ages</u> *(a funny workbook for kids of all ages also available on Lulu)* and let it play with your mind and fulfill your heart and engage you in the arts for ages!

Hopefully this person who bought my book "by accident" or by distraction will benefit from some (if not all) of my words in there. They usually give an insight to those who read them. After all, making a book by one's own hands and writing one have things in common, and the most important and essential is the love one has for books and for Art in general. So it was not a mistake after all!

SPIRITUAL ALZHEIMER

If you enjoyed this, you might be interested in the following blogs (if you Google my name you will find them too):
Dance As One
Orbs
And I will be much obliged if you send me a word or two on Twitter, even if only to tell me about YOUR dreams:
@AnaBowlova
Thank YOU!
****

So How To Become More Spiritual Awaked?

 Thanksgiving is that time of the year that makes you reflect upon the things that you should be thankful for in your life. But have you ever really had your thoughts turning on to people instead of things? If you didn't do this shift in your head yet, you should try this for now on.

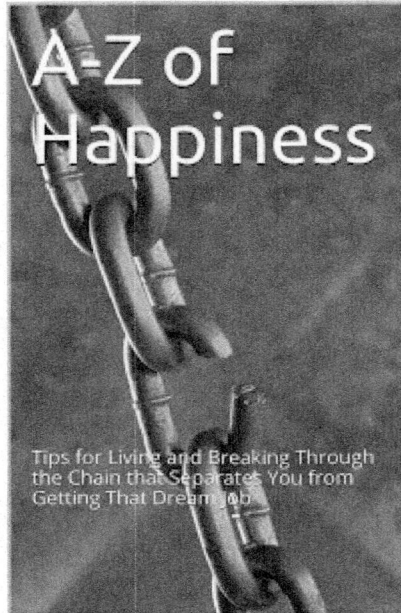

I recently published the book <u>A-Z of Happiness: Tips to Live By</u> <u>and Break Through the Chains that Keeps You from Getting that</u> <u>Dream Job</u> which I wrote to help so many fellow friends who needed a push to increase their chances of getting a job out there while finding happiness in their inner core. I go through the whole alphabet explaining on what is keeping you from living your life to the fullest. If you didn't read my book go get a copy, the tips I leave there are worth the two cents. I assure you after reading it you will turn from larvae to a butterfly. And if you don't you should give it two more shots in your head (no, not literally), but by giving you two more chances, for I am a believer that you should try things "thrice" before turning things away. And again, that's THE THING: It's a good way to show you that YOU should change your perspective on things.

SPIRITUAL ALZHEIMER

Just to list a few examples with the rule of three, thus in the same way that I wrote my book:

- You are thankful for the new found. Instead of thinking of numbers, think not about friendships, but of each one of your new **friends** to whom you devote yourself and feel so grateful, all people who you may have encountered along the way.
- You are thankful for **life**. Well, that seems too generic. Don't think of life as a thing, but as you, you living your life, not life living (or leaving) you. That meaning YOU, not your life for what you should be thankful. Don't separate you from the most important part/subject of yourself: **You**, **Life**!
- Now you should be thankful for **laughing**, and again, there was a reason about what you to be laughing. And it was not a thing; it was someone deep inside who makes you laugh. If not from an source, it was not something from the exterior, as this force that motivated you to laughing came from **within**, it (trans)forms in an **ulterior** reason, and again if you are thinking of a thing, which is not... guess who, not what!

Thankful for **doing** what you believe in, but doing is stuff made outside of you. Think rather of **being**, and you will feel it deep inside as a truth that resonates inside of you.

The Mysterious Murder of MM

You thought as this day to be any **ordinary, common** day. This day will never occur again, everything that happens today, even the clouds in the sky, they won't be there tomorrow. So don't think of transient things. Think of who will endure; this way you will focus on the **essential, the essence** of being. **People** are people. Things are things: Did you see what I did there? People come first. And period. People beat themselves down, especially (or if only) on Thanksgiving Day for taking things for granted, when they should be praised for doing exactly that.

It is not things that matter anyone anyway. People who matter, living beings are the ones who matter. And every time you think of things as people, you miss the point. Instead of people per se, the thing is of material stuff; or living beings, such as your dog, your cat, a parrot, a bird that insists to wake you up every morning so you don't be late for work, a neighbor who sings her lungs out for she wants to be part of an Opera, and this one is not me, to be clear (*clearing my throat). So every time you turn beings into things a star stops blinking in the sky and an angel dies in Heaven. That last statement was just to scare you out! (Although I do believe in angels, they won't die because you don't believe in them, anyway!)

So don't be thankful for **thing**s... for Go(^l^)ds sake!
And have a nice Thanksgiving **Day... every single day**!

SPIRITUAL ALZHEIMER

The deep meditation keeps the stress levels diminished to the point of altering the action of hormones on the brain, causing a relaxation beneficial to the whole nervous system. Even people who suffer from a traumatic event keep less trauma collateral effects. And they are calmer and are more able to deal with it with considerable ease and go on with their lives thanks to constant states of relaxation.

Meditation works more and better than a full night's sleep. That's because the brain levels are still there when in a sleep state more accelerated than when in a state of meditation, and the more there is the habit of meditating deeply over, more the body learns to recover from the stress which means more life, energy and creativity in their activities. To meditate does not necessarily that you have to be at rest, even in a pretty hectic activity one can meditate. Be amazed then! That's right! Even as someone is looking agitated from the outside one can reach an impressive level of meditation.

And there is a tale that takes place in a monastery:
"Master, are you meditating?" a monk asks his master who is sitting with eyes closed. To which the master replied, "No, I'm working." He then gets up and goes to the garden and starts weeding the land. When the disciple sees his master sweating in full physical activity he falls into an assumption and conclusion. "Oh, and now, are you working?" the pupil asks him. The teacher focused on his activity and without stop working the land with his hoe, smiles back at him as he keeps weeding. "Now I am meditating." He simply says.

So here below I leave my video channel link. If you search under the list *Animation* you will find that this is where I captured images that can help you achieve a level of active meditation with considerable relaxing effect.

http://www.youtube.com/user/anabowlova

8

COMIC CONS-PIRACY

If I wrote this book as a non-fiction you wouldn't believe the things that I'm saying here anyway... or would you? So let's keep it light and move up with the conspiracy theories.

It's the beginning of the year 2015, and just one week after so many explosions and bursts of gunpowder meaning the fireworks all around the world, coloring the skies with magical designs, and Allah is once again on the scene.

"Je Suis Charlie!" The Parisian "Hebdomadaire" (a weekly journal) Charlie Hebdo got attacked by four gunmen who supposedly said they belong to Al-Qaeda and went inside the Newspaper Building to kill ten cartoonists and a policeman. And the whole world is terrified by their actions. Freedom of speech by all costs! Now being this a fiction let's say Al-Qaeda is a non-existent organization, something created by you-must-now-know-who. That's a well-planned crime, a very cheap but prove to be useful way of manipulating the masses to believe in a war.

"I guess that's a George Orwell's novel 1984 all over." Someone else said.

110

"Faites l'humour, pas la guerre!" Or rather "Haga Humor, No la Guerra." A Chilean (or French, I'm not even sure anymore) cartoonist writes... (Or draws?) Humor in cartoon is after all a weapon of mass creation. In a satirical, critical, witty way they can depict the truth without sounding so serious and crude as the truth may often become.

"Make Laughter not War!" I repeat. Those killers were the ones to confound slaughter with laughter. And unfortunately the cartoonists were just another collateral damage, such as many who didn't survive from the falling of the towers.

And yet by the next week of the slaughter *Charlie Hebdo* that for years had been suffering a severe financial crisis went out with (what was initially a million) three million copies in sixteen languages for the survival edition shipped and gone! Yes, they were all gone in a few seconds and they made two million more copies... No wait. A quick update: now they are seven million copies around the globe.

"Tout est pardonne!" It says in the cover of this historical edition that had people making lines and who came from all parts and went from miles to miles to buy it.

"Everything is forgiven..." is written in the cover. And it's forgotten very freakish easily too!

And all this commotion and homage around the world also will soon be vanished in a type of collective amnesia. People just don't question much about things anymore, they go with the flow. France did indeed try to warn about the "terror spectacular" being implemented and just after that the country became entangled by myriads of terror suspects and attacks. So that's the real tragedy of it all if you put it in magnified lenses. Surrendered by what seems bigger than any government response of an ethical action, they simply go with the flow, the end result being the total collapse of the EU. And soon after or even before I publish this book chances are that all this issue about freedom of speech and such will be totally forgotten. And so it is!

But then the secret organizations that orchestrated that entire circus already got what they want.

The entire establishment is corrupted to an end: they want to perpetuate the frontiers closed and a perpetual sense of fear and insecurity towards all citizens will be spread in the USA and the European Union (now des-union) like a dis-ease, that´s right, people won´t feel at ease and there will be a constant neighbor´s watching.

And that´s so much easier to catch than the deadly Ebola, being this although even more dangerous and invisible to the ordinary human beings accommodated on building fences in their own houses to their utopian defenses and constructing indestructible walls in their brains. And then they are so ready to be mentally controlled by a few other manipulative minds.

And talking about walls and castles made in sand and spilled actions; all we see in the sea of lies now is that the oil prices are still declining. Funny enough, not long ago oil was considered scarce and the prices were reaching higher and higher. Now it´s so cheap, that would soon be cheaper than water. A way of breaking the BRICK, with now Korean flag in the block, as this news didn´t pass the public view and didn´t make the headlines:

"Early Saturday morning (6 December 2014), President Hollande was in route to Paris from his state visit to Kazakhstan when his plane requested an immediate/emergency flight path deviation to Moscow's Vnukovo International Airport (VIA) where the French leader "requested/demanded" that he be met by Putin upon his landing.

Upon President Hollande's arrival at VIA, he was escorted with his security/intelligence entourage to the government's Terminal 2 facilities "safe room" that protects its occupants from electronic surveillance.

Upon Putin's "rushed arrival" and meeting with his French counterpart at the VIA, GRU analysts in this report say, a "visibly distraught" President Hollande began detailing how his countries DGSE had informed him of their uncovering of an Obama regime plot to stage a massive false flag terror attack which the blame of which would be placed on Russia."

And in this case the blame was Putin, I mean, put in the

extremists.

Sanctions or War... So THAT's the question... Seriously? Syria is the target now with this terrorism attack in Paris. But let's go back to the Boston Marathon attack two years ago, and you see some similarities, with the same M.O.: They were two brothers; the terrorists in Paris left an ID (very convenient) so apropos for the police to find out that they were two Muslims brothers too, infiltrated in the society. They were cells who acted like normal people but ready anytime when "activated". If that's not a brainwash or an implant in the brain...

There is even a cartoonist who supported the ones who were killed in the attack, drawing a somewhat similar scene referring to the September eleven attacks, which instead of the twin towers it was showing two pencils in place and an airplane just about to hit them both. An airplane in the Twin Tower makes the symbol A11 or 911, which in turn means All or Apollo 11, all symbols of only one group, one organized crime instigating fear to people to establish a New World Order.

To quote the quotes in the writings of a destroyed human mind manipulated by the elite that made us (represented by Jack Nicholson's character) in Kubrick's (and yes, yet another "Cube Brick") movie "The Shinning" all like a machine (and notice that his son in the movie wears a blouse with a neat knitted Apollo 11 drawing):

"All work and no play make Jack a dumb boy..." Okay, so vain and insane!

You may also find Stanley Kubrick Exposition at the Museum of Image and Sound: in Sao Paulo through *my youtube channel:* http://www.youtube.com/user/anabowlova

Kubrick who also created a whole scenario in the outer space with his *2001 Odyssey of Space* also had made with the same technique a whole new story around "the men in the moon who came down too soon". Let me tell you, that's such a mind blowing! And that also takes us back to Marilyn Monroe assassins.

"What the heck MM has to do with all this?" you might as well ask.

Those are the same responsible for her to be shut up because she knew about them. They are the same ones who manipulate the masses and make a president their puppet today.

"There is no way to take it slightly, or to start pounding this down like M&M's. And MM (I mean Marilyn Monroe and not the double check Marx & MaoTse-Tung) had so hit the nail in the head. There was something that she knew since then and it continues to be that way up to this day. Nothing changed and I mean anything at all."

"Anything at all... again the word "all" or A11... And what did not change?" I ask. I'm afraid I have been misled down to here.

"That all nations are bankrupt names in business ruled by corrupted minds. That they have a Geo-physical weapon which includes the modification of weathers, whether would it be to cause no rain in some areas while devastating other parts with flood, or fire, hurricanes, earthquakes, chem-trails, bio-tech, check, tic-tact, tack, etc. And she was about to reveal all that too when she was cowardly murdered. And we still cannot see the strings that pull the ball..."

"A man made hurricane... what the hurry, Citizen Kane?"

"Rosebud..." said Kane before he died.

"That's right, put that in the records!"

"And what we ought to do with all this info here??"

Pocket up the best and shake out the rest.

And the day came when the butterfly broke up from its cocoon because staying inside proved to be way too painful

"Je suis Charlie!" It was written everywhere. That phrase was spread during the whole ordeal as it had been alleged that the terrorists, upon entering the building, asked an employee, "Qui est Charlie?" Who was Charlie? As they were looking for the director of the journal whose name was Stephane Charbonnier but he was better known as Charb. Already suffering many threats, he said that he would rather die standing up then down on his knees. In his last cartoon he wrote the words: "(It's 2015 and) we don't have any terrorist attacks in France yet?" And he drew a terrorist saying, "Wait! We still have until the end of January to make our vows of a New Year!" And exactly one week after the New Year celebration they were cruelly assassinated the director and four cartoonists among their colleagues. And they were all "Charlie" for they all played a role in that weekly charge magazine.

"And the day came when the risk to remain tight in a bud was more painful than the risk it took to blossom" Anaïs Nin

He had a nervous breakdown after his stepmother had decided to marry a Turkish billionaire that she had just met at a client's wedding that she had to attend in Ibiza. The American bride, actually her father, had paid for her expenses, for the bride wanted to wear a wedding dress in the same fashion as Marilyn Monroe did when she sang "Happy Birthday" for the president. There were real diamonds supposed to fit in every thread, and she had to sew the fabric directly into the bride's body. And she was Queen size. Hours of labor were spent before the ceremony. But well worth applied for that it implied her to meet a billionaire. Dawson thought his stepmother's heart belonged to him and after she found out a substitute for such volatile feeling, he started taking Zoloft ever since. He became wild. Now he lives in a Zoo loft. Really! It's a loft that they built for him, right inside the Zoo, in order for him to keep a 24/7 job routine, no sleeping and always working, feeding the animals at the National Park. That's what the jury decided in his case as a form of penalty before taking him into imprisonment. That's until he joined the monkeys and started throwing peanuts at the public.

Well, that was way before he got shot and was killed by the police anyway. And if you think that police force in Brazil or in the US, well, in the majority of the countries in all Americas is violent, I've got only two words for you...

Jean Charles!

"Dawson's dead, Dawson's dead!" A parrot cried out loud.

"Damn son is dad... Damn so is dad..." the monkeys repeated the bird, in a mockery, agitated in their own cages.

Dawson was her half-brother AND her father at the same time. And in spite of their ages difference, he was nineteen when she was born, Christie didn't stop having feelings for him. She always felt so close to him... And that was exactly why he couldn't marry her. They were way too close. It was so much so, that they shared the same blood. It was the biggest top secret that her mother kept from her. And if you find it hard to conceive (and no pun intended) that a parent would fall in love with a foster child, again I've got only two words for you: Woody Allen.

And now he was dead. Dawson, I mean, her dad. And if added to that, her mother's tongue was a tomb. This big secret was now buried with him for good....

....Or for bad, too bad! His stepmother forbade him of saying a word. She would never forgive him if he spilled that out, for Christie sake.

Now she could finally breath in a sigh of relief. Her secret was then very well-kept six feet under.

He died just like Jean Charles... the Brazilian young man who was cowardly murdered in England, shot six times in the head, dead by the London Police Department in a somewhat weird persecution. Just after that they would find out that he was no terrorist and that he carried no gun or any kind of weapon over his backpack. The same police that we had in Brazil, which by the way was trained by the British intelligence, the ones still in the age of stone; they first shoot then ask. We are living a civil war, or we just don´t know it yet.

She couldn't believe her eyes. He tried to run away from the police while being transferred to another prison and now he was dead. It all happened the same afternoon, just after she left that psychic place. Oh, he was dead, and she still cannot believe that!

She mourned his death like a widow would do. She wore black for the next five months after that horrendous accident. Christie kept the picture on her mind's eye of him running from the two policemen as they were still trying to stop him. He fell on the ground, they tried to grab him, and then... She heard a shot. And after that, everything looked dark in her mind.

Christie goes back in a tunnel to the days when they were still dating. She hadn't seen him for ages. He looked as old as his father and now he stood in the middle of the street right there where he got shot on his chest. She was wondering how much of heartbreak he could take anyway. He missed her that much. After a big fight they had gone to a coffeehouse. They waited on line.

"Are you together?" The attendant asked.

"Not for long!" Christie said.

At this freaking party a man gave her a bunch of herbs to smoke. She neglected him.

He took her hand and he pulled up a white powder over her nose. She didn't want to inhale that thing that he kept pulling in her nostrils. And there she breathed that substance inside her lungs. And she could not help anymore, as she opened her mouth and he closed it instead, with his teeth chewing her lips, yet she had to breathe. His mouth was soft as cotton and it had a sweet taste.

"I cannot breathe... I cannot breathe!" She said as he kept pounding the powder over her nose and his tongue over her throat.

Christie was way too high to care about what was really happening. She lost her senses and she became part of the ritual. She completely gave up fighting against that man who insisted on making her inhale the white stuff and she was about to fain when she heard a sharp and intense cry.

A tall long haired man came and kissed her. He pressed his both hands over her chest and inserted his entire tongue on her mouth. Now he pulled her tongue out.

"He doesn't have the nerve to treat me like a doll..." she thought in a state of shock. " I cannot move and he doesn't really care if he is hurting me..."

"Hey, what are you doing?" Christie finally said, looking

desperately right into his eyes. She thought that he could hear what she was saying then. But the fact was that she could not spell a word, if she was the one under a spell.

She heard another cry of a higher pitch penetrating in the dark.

She looked around. Everybody looked like they were moving in a kind of slow motion dance, but now they seemed to be part of an electrical parade. The whole floor shook as she tried to balance herself up and she felt the floor trembling like an earthquake, as she could not feel the earth beneath her feet. She was totally taken under the effects of a hallucinatory and revolutionary commotion. And only that dread and vertiginous sensation remained.

"The girl is dead!"

The police would arrive soon.

"What are they talking about?" Christie was about to have a sort of mental breakdown. She started to shiver and looked at all directions searching for a clue of what was really going on. "I must have lost the whole scene!"

"Her name is Cindy Ferraz..." a girl with a pink lace in a pony tail told her. She was wearing a polka dot dress matching her white shoes with black dots, in a shocking check-mate like playing a game of chess. Her red-blondish hair was so thick that she had often stuck her pinky fake nails around it to keep the lace in her ponytail up. And her hips balanced her dress side by side, as she casually passed by and walked through the ballroom. She almost burst into laughter as she kept reporting the incident as a mere occasional situation. "Like Cinderella, she came so beautifully dressed, and she even sang with that rapper."

"And now she is a total wrap," the long haired guy said.

"She took some drugs, and she started to have slight seizures which lead her to a serious epileptic attack. I think that she had an overdose.... she was vomiting her lungs out of her chest."

"I know her!" The girl with the pink lace continued to say that to anyone who would question what happened. As if that knowledge would add her flair and give her a touch of glamour.

"She is a model-slash-actress-slash-singer-slash-dancer and she was about to finish another Colombian Soap Opera."

But how the heck she ended up like that?

"You killed her?" Christie yelled at them in a desperate look, while a man tried to force the exit and leave the place.

They stopped. They could not force their way out of the building. Right in front of the door there was a yellow tape all around it wrapping and trapping them to remain inside.

The police arrived. It was already too late to attempting an escapade. They started to make questions to the whole group.

Christie tried to leave and started to sneak out of the room where the ritual was set, but one of the policemen there grabbed her arm. She forced her way out to escape from his hand as she intended to run away as fast as she could, even if for that she had to leave her hand behind.

"Wait a minute there, young lady! Where do you think you are going?" said another man inside a black car, with a pale face like a ghost,. He reached her as she tried her way out.

"Ah! I don't know anything about it. Just let me go!"

The police officer stood in front of her, hurting her as he grabbed her hand in a very forceful way. He saw that she was about to beat him hard and then he pulled her closer to him, raising her skirt opening her legs wide, leaving them spread close to him. She tried to get away from the lace that the cop formed with his hands over her waist, while he retained her with his body against her back. And as he pulled her closer and closer against him, she could smell the plastic material from his new uniform. She could feel his breath too: such a stench that was coming from his mouth….

"Let me go!" It was a horrendous odor in an arduous night. Her head was in a whirl.

A man in his early thirties, wearing a leather coat, with a skin as soft as a gentle soap, touched her arm and disengaged her from the other officer's hands, and he disarmed her with his smile. She looked at him; he was tall and had the most charming face

"Let her go!" He said as he showed her his badge. She jumped between the two of them and reached out towards the exit.

"Don´t be afraid!" he said as he grabbed a cold beer from the bar. He came towards her and held her up a foot from the floor. The other policeman just held her in the other side, supporting his companion.

"How come?" She said while still trying to disengage from them both. She swept her arms up and down, making circles in the air in an attempt to get rid of the brutes.

"Thirsty?" He offered her a sip of beer from his glass.

She turned his glass downward and splashed the whole beer over his face making him be obliged to let herself go. He set the empty glass over the bar and flashed his badge once again over her face.

"Trust me, I work for the Government."

Christie was still trying to escape when he grabbed her arm back to him, as he was holding her until she gave up fighting.

"We won´t hurt you." He said looking right into her eyes.

"How am I supposed to believe that if you already hurt me?"

He slowed her down, as he kept his badge scrubbed over her face. She then noticed that he was supposedly a detective.

Christie was still incredulous. He looked at her face and smiled once again. She could not help and she smiled right back at his silver grayish eyes. She could barely hear his voice of a strong soft and mild tone all at the same time.

"What is your name, sweetie?"

She didn't say a word.

"Cat cut your tongue?" said the other officer.

Was she afraid of saying her name and revealing her ID?

"Oh, I forgot my name…" She was not kidding after all. Christie was so overwhelmed by the whole scenario that she completely forgot who she was only for a few seconds. A few seconds only… then she was back on track. But the detective was simply following instructions and the tactics to get information which he had learned a long ago in his years of practice back at

Quantico, in Virginia.

"Did you know that girl?"

"Not particularly, no! But she is famous, isn't she?"

A silence. What a dreadful silence. He would not talk. She just wanted to go back home. He made notes in a white sheet.

"She was strangulated..."

"Oh, my... But I thought...I mean, they said...she had an overdose..." Christie looked like a contortionist, tweaking her eyebrow, turning her face and neck to one side and her upper body to the other side, her hips shaking side to side. She was confused, with a twisted mind overwhelmed by the whole event.

"Who is here to help you? Is there anybody to take you home?"

She looked around trying to find her boyfriend, but he was long gone.

"Look, baby. I am not going to take you into prison; you didn't do anything. At least, that is what I believe. If you don't tell me who you are, or show me any ID, I will have to take you to the police department and start to ask you questions while you have a cup of coffee to clear up your mind, do you understand?"

"Well, I do understand...." She thought.

"Cup of coffee sounds not bad..." that was the only phrase that she could come up with.

They took her to the police department.

"You were totally intoxicated... full of narcotics in that party... I was the guy who saved you..."

"Hey, wait!" Christie disengaged her arm from his hand. "I am still trying to make sense from the first phrase that you spelled out...I intoxicated? Were you the tall long haired guy making a mouth-to-mouth procedure... the one who saved me?" Her thoughts were running as fast as a thunder in her head.

"So we've been tailing me..." The detective comically shook the long haired wig that he managed to have tailored like a tail as he kept it tucked inside his pants behind him. He touched his chest mimicking a surprise. "I'm feeling a little busted now." And she didn't even notice his prank. She was still trying to keep up not to lose her train of thoughts.

"What do you mean by that? I didn't take any drug..."

"Someone gave you a white powder and you sniffed it in almost to a fatal collapse. Only if I didn't sniff you out on time..."

"I didn't see that coming," she said. "So I did indeed inhale the thing up. I do not even remember smelling any-shin..."

"That is their idea. Drug dealers want YOU to get high, without even noticing it," said the detective in a pompous tone.

"As for them, they don't really experiment none of that stuff."

The detective felt completely at ease as he explained his day-to-day occurrences and activities that he was most used to get in his routine experiences.

"They never try it! They do not care about you. They care simply about them, and forget about your health as you pay with your life."

"Here it goes. I didn't see that coming neither. That is all that I was waiting for: a lecture in the middle of those people at the police department. Oh, that's great!" Christie was becoming really impatient. To have that friendly cup of coffee that he had promised her seemed the only thing that kept her from collapsing her entire body on the ground and burying her whole being inside a hole.

"I just feel so stupid!"

She looked around. She looked in the mirror that stayed strong and firm on the wall after what seemed like a hurricane right in front of her. Her eyes were red and burning, and she ran with them, rolling them side by side to see if she could still move them. She quirked them quickly up and down and she made a complete circle around the orbits as fast as she could, the way that she desired that her whole body would move as well. At least that is what she should be doing right then.

"Run! And I could run as fast as I can without fainting. Can I really make it?"

But she still kept her head down, looking at the floor. There was a red-yellowish liquid all over it, running like blood. It was actually blood currently running with a current of thoughts and poisoned fluids eager to take over her whole body, as a distillate wine tickling frenetically through her veins in a dreadful pain.

"Puff!" She panted.

"What a mess of cultures in this building! I wonder if it is always like that in the police station: This multicultural festival of people. I bet it is always like that, since I live in a place, which is full of presence of people from different cultures, and different beliefs."

That's America, the land of cultural contrasts, diversities and opportunities.

"Where is the handsome that "saved" me?" Christie grasped. He was not there anymore. What a shame…

"Hey, where is my coffee?" She finally asked.

When they finally released her, she breathed completely relieved as she relived the entire night. The moon was already there watching her over the sky when she left the building.

It was just then that she remembered that she had left her cellular phone in her car. She put her hands on her head as she felt her brains were about to explode with the blood coming back to its circuits.

"Man! Where did I leave my car? Oh, boy… What a night!"

She walked encompassed in the streets of Philadelphia. She stopped at the supermarket to get some food. It was already close. Christie didn´t give up in her quest.

"The refrigerator must be empty."

She headed home as fast as she could but not before grabbing a sandwich at seven-eleven nearby Jefferson Station in the Market Street. No sign of any police behind her back... She sighed. She could finally take a rest.

She arrived home. She looked for her key inside her purse. She heard some steps behind her. Someone just passed near her. She hurried up and grabbed the key to just let it fall back again.

"Oh, that´s so hard to find the door key when you most need it inside this black hole!" A "black hole" is how she called her purse.

She finally inserted the key in the hole and gently wiggled it.

The door lock was jammed and needed extra care. When she finally opened it she looked around before she entered to make sure no one was waiting behind her or had been following her. She took out her clothes and was going directly to the shower without even noticing that she had left her front door ajar. She was about to soak her whole body with soap when she remembered to go look at her voice mail panel first.

There was a red sign dancing like a fool on that white electronic apparel. That reminded of herself dancing her way out as the police officer grabbed her from behind and talked to her with that foul smell coming from his mouth. That gave her the chills.

"Oh, well...no messages...what the heck is Dawson, anyway? He disappeared! That son of a dawn...."

Beep!

"Hey, honey, where have you been? I was worried about you. You disappeared and I left the place before the cops...you know...that tragedy, and then..."

She quickly grabbed the telephone receiver.

"Where have I been?" She answered to that metal-icy voice on the other side of the line.

"You are so cynical! You left me there so do not come with excuses..."

"Hey, baby, so, you are home. Good Lord, what happened to you? You disappeared over the crowd..."

"No baby, YOU disappeared! I was looking' for you, and you left the ground...you left me there all by myself!"

"Did you see what happened? I think the girl was a Latin bitch...and then, the cops arrived..."

"Yeah, the cops arrived, they handcuffed me and they almost took me in prison...you were the one who got me into that...I am so mad! I am so..."

She hung up the phone. She was too angry to complete the conversation. The carpet was totally wet. She had left a trail of blood mixed with soapy water behind her when she went to get the phone.

Just then that she noticed that she had been hurt. And that was not the work of the policeman.

Christie was too high then to even notice this.

One of the guys who were there at the ritual grabbed her while she was drugged and he took advantage of her trance and cut the inner side of her leg with a small knife as he tried to tear up her underwear. And she didn't even remember that before.

She got another phone call. It was the handsome policeman. She was too tired to talk on the phone.

This time she let the machine get the message for her.

"Hello. This is Officer Smith. I would like to make an appointment with you, to check out more about the case report. Please give me a call at: 966 6894. Thank you."

Beep!

Christie collapsed on her bed as soon as she got some sleeping pills. She spread the pills through her mouth.

"Need some beer though to get them down on my throat." She stood up still groggy and went tottering to the refrigerator. It was just then that she had noticed that she had left her front door open. She reached the door with difficulty, almost crawling towards it, and she closed it with one turn of the key. She felt weak. She looked at her hand. There were bruised all over her wrist. It had been almost one hour after that incident and she could not still take that girl's face over thy/my (dyed-died) head.

"Ts-ts", the woman said in disapproval of those children playing so freely in front of her, almost like an affront to her decency. Years gone and she couldn't take back. And she was evil enough to make a spell to those lovely care-free kids.

"Oh, how much I miss my childhood... Then when I would play with the other girls, and teach them about rhythms while I clasped my hands as fast as I could, and they could not follow me and it was so funny. "

Then she jumped with her head going up and down as she remembered her going between two ropes while the other girls bounced them like swirling snakes covering her whole body and enveloping her like waves in the ocean.

'But then I was so much younger, and I had so many more dreams as I believed I had to follow my bliss... I was so naive. I didn't care for the things of the adulthood...and why should I care anyway?

Even when that witch (bitch) woman told us when she saw those so free-from-stress girls playing:

"You play all you want now. Seize your childhood, before it is gone...because, baby, those years pass fast and soon they will be gone forever!" Since the day that I have paid attention to those words, I stopped playing.'

Her mind took her back to her American School that she had left with so many dreams and goals to accomplish. The school was founded by a Methodist Priest.

"And you know what they say about the Methodists, that they are methodical and like illustrative examples. After all, do you know how many Methodist it takes to change a light bulb?" she asked to herself. She was talking nonsensically in delirium.

"That's under-termed: Whether the light is clean, dim and deemed, or completely screwed, you ARE love, no matter how brewed! Let me drink first to swallow the rest of this stuff down on my throat."

"Cheers!"

She heard a celestial bell; it was a sound out of this world, like an angel timber, that woke her up at exactly ten minutes after nine o'clock.

There she was in Philadelphia. *Philos* meaning love and *Delphos* gods. There where the gods meet love. The city of gods' love and that's what it means Philadelphia? She grabbed the phone.

"Mom, something terrible happened..."

"Oh, my! What did you do, Christina?"

"I didn't do anything! Just that Dawn... son of a gun..."

"Oh, boy! What did he do this time? Oh, don't tell me that you got married and you forgot to invite me..." she said, with a giggle and a nervous laughter.

"No, mom, I told you that I would never marry any man... My heart belongs to..."

"...me! Yeah, yeah! You told me that, Misses Murphy! Please, sugar, do not do anything wrong. You had just moved away from me. Did you find a job yet?"

"No, mom, but I am going to go to another interview today. Listen, I have to go now..."

"But what happened, Chris? Are you not going to tell me something? Nothing at all?"

"Oh, mom...I will tell you later...no big deal..."

"...no big deal? You were almost crying!"

"No, mom, that is okay. It was another fight that we were having...Dawson and I... I don't know about him... I think that I will break up with him..."

"But again? How many times do I have to hear that? You will end up marrying this guy, oh, ho...I am sure of that!"

"Got to go, mom!" she interrupted her mother who was almost crying on the phone.

"Hey, mom, I really got to go... talk to you a later..."

Then she heard a sigh on the other side of the line... a deadline made them rush to get things straight as soon as possible.

She made another call. This time it was Art to whom she had been calling. He turned his eyes on the other line and thus did not pay much attention to her. He always did that anyway, even when they were face-to-face, he would never be looking directly to her, but to the other way around, never looking directly to her eyes and seeing her completion that in a way also disturbed him so very much. And he could not see as tears were coming falling from her eyes.

"I am so overwhelmed by that entire incident at that party..."

Christie thought that she was speaking to him, when in fact it was just her imagination, just through her conscience that she could hear herself talking.

"I better not tell him", she said. "I need to spare him from this disgust; he already has so much going on in his life...after his father in prison who murdered his own wife. He was in an orphaned home, and now his grandparents who don't give a shit for him...Oh, well, I better not tell him, no, no!"

She turned her face out to look around, afraid that someone would be watching her. It was a misty night and it didn't seem that it would get much better than that. People looked gray; they all wore black coats and seemed to defeat the early winter approaching so quickly, the hush-hush of the whole situation and the rush wind without the fall defying its harshness.

"You look tired..."

"Who, me? Yeah, I am tired!"

"I better get going...You go get some rest."

"Ok, I'd rather, for that's better than getting someone arrested!" She said.

He pulled the chair for her. She touched his hand and stood up carefully.

"Have a good one!" He said as she let him take her hand up to kiss it in a casual yet theatrical way.

"Oh, I would die with his chivalry." She said to herself. Her legs trembled just while thinking of his romantic way, and his gentleman mannerisms that almost often and completely drove her crazy, something so rare nowadays. And that he would make the most obvious in his soul.

"Oh, how I desire him. How I wish I could feel the least fragrance of his kiss in my lips, and feel the tenderness of his embrace. If he could just know... just know how much I desire him. I am going to kick Dawson out, and stay with him in his castle of love." She completed her statement without even noticing that he looked at her right at that moment when she let it skip the word "love" out of her mind.

He smiled at her...

"You pretty bastard..."

"What?" He asked.

"Oh, I said, you look pretty... mastered so well on your outfit, Art..."

And then she just touched his Calvin Klein's jeans. And then again he seemed abstract to any touch that she could give to his skin. That's what disarmed her most. The individual flame that she felt from him and the electrical current that surpassed their bodies when they were together and that he didn't even notice that it existed between them.

"Art, how come you stole my heart, that I could never marry any other man, but you? If you could only know what is inside my heart.... But I am afraid."

She was afraid that the revelation that she eagerly want to share with him would scare him to death and that she would never see him again. He would escape to the furthest lands of this world.

"And our love would be doomed forever. I'd rather suffer in silence, than to risk of losing his friendship."

She knew about how fragile his anima was, and how tender was his soul. She knew that she was playing with fire and that he was just a fish swimming among sharks in murky water. The shapeless, that it seemed the serpent of the sea made it more complicated to touch it. The streams could easily loose the course.

And the vibration that started small can became of a bigger radiance. It could leave an avalanche of trembling lines that danced in the lakes but it never stopped.

"I do not want to wait in vain for your love..."

"You've got such a beautiful voice. You never thought about becoming a singer?"

"Me, a singer? Ha, Art! You hurt me. Please ... Enough that I already disturbed the girls of the choral that I made part. I am too loud!"

"But that is the thing. You were born to be a star, to make a single solo. Not to make your voice be confounded between so many tones. You just lose yourself when you think you are less than you are supposed to be, little girl!"

Oh. Little girl! Oh, yeah, that is who she was for him... just a little girl ready for a play.

"I don't want to wait in vain for your love..."

Annie Lennox was still playing over and over in her head.

How tender was his smile. But he stopped smiling as soon as he saw that she smiled back at him, as if he was afraid of losing his pride. He pulled the chair for her again. And she fell right into the tip of the chair. He grabbed her before she fell on the floor. How not to fall for a man like him?

"Thanks, Art!" He pushed the chair back to the position where the seat sees under the table and thoroughly knows the table's entire secret.

And the table doesn't even need to say what's going on.

"Hum-hum!" He responded, eventually, in a very casual manner.

"Don't you see, stupid? That I am in love with you? How come you treat me like an acquaintance if I know you since I was nine?"

His black and shinny hair became a lightning blue against the pearled moon light. Oh, he looked even more charming with the rays of the silvery touching against his skin.

His eyes had that mysterious look of someone who lived awhile awake and never conceived to live in the darkness. Did he have some sleep? His passion seemed to be an amalgam of love and the enormous heart he had.... Did he have a heart? Of course, he did! His heart was beating for the two of them, it was within her! Her Art...

"Excuse-me?"

"What?" she said.

"Did I hear it clearly? You said "my Art"?"

"Did I say it too loud that he heard it?" she asked to herself, doubting about the power of her passion that it was so loud like a thunder in a heavy cloud in a dark sky.

"No, I said, my heart...yeah, my heart! Oh, my heart is going to explode if I do not calm down, and relax."

"Chris, let me call you a cab. You look tired. You must go take a nap now."

"I will, I will."

After that, he simply disappeared. She took a five-minute nap.

During her sleep she heard a bell ringing again, with that same celestial timber that she had listened for the past few months, as if a thousand angels touched it, as if announcing the end of a dreadful time and the return of the dead to their places.

"For whom the bell tolls?"

"It tolls for you!"

She woke up, and looked at the watch: it was nine eleven again, at the same time that she had called her mother, only that her watch was suffering a jet lag; it was marking the time in the South hemisphere still. She put her ear over it. She heard no beat. There is no tic-tact.

That is more like brick-a-brace than a bric-a-brac; and it was simply not working anymore...

She felt as if something was trying to say that it was time to go to the police office and try to get this out of her neck once and for all. She takes courage and calls the detective who had already said that he would be working overnight.

"Need some information about the Juniper Street's case."

"Juniper? Oh, I've got it! That is the name of the street where the incident happened."

"That's exactly right!"

"See, I do not even know exactly where I was... Don't bother..." O Brother Where Art Thou?

"And how are you doing, by the way?"

"Listen, we need you here right away."

"Oh, well, what the hell. I better go there. Sooner or later I will have to do that, anyway."

Meanwhile, the coffee was waiting for her at the Starbucks. She got a nice cup of Mocha and left to the office.

She got into her car and drove as if she was an automaton. She could not stop thinking about the scene of that man touching that girl's tongue and pulling it out, so that she would not swallow it. There in her mind it ran the same film. She could not stop visualizing that half-human, half-super hero making a mouth-to-mouth revival on her. And she still felt all that hot breath inside her chest filling out her lungs from his miraculous air.

She arrived at the building, which happened to be near her place. It took a long time to find a place to park her car. She finally spotted a spot in the parking lot.

It took a while too until she can finally talk to that "god". He was tall man and he owned the most beautiful white teeth that she had ever seen. His smile transported her to another world.

He was a detective, right! But his distinctive *savior-faire* towards her and his badge didn't show the real character under that black coat. He looked like the hero in a mystery novel. He exhaled such an exotic fragrance, a mixture of lust and desire and a passion that could easily being detected by any sensitive person. He transpired, and a lot, but what he exhaled was pure seduction and adrenaline.

He was so particularly careful with his attitude that he was easily recognized by the emotional eye of a girl full of love for adventure. And she was also fascinated by his deep feelings inside his eyes.

She was quite overly emotional right then, and so vulnerable and it seemed as if he took advantage of her dreamlike state to make her fall into his spells.

The litigated lunar satisfaction seems too small in retrospect to the indication of a flesh soul. His connection to a pagan ritual can hardly disguise his excuse for an interrogation. In the hall at that courtroom, he knelt down next to her and almost begged her to tell him the truth.

But how could she reveal what was inside her mind, if all that she could do for him there was to completely open up her heart? She was totally overwhelmed by the entire situation.

"Can I have that cup of coffee you so promised to me right now?" She said almost breathless.

Maybe coffee could break up his spell, which seemed like a course turning her inside out from all over her soul.

"No coffee now. We need some information, and we need you clean."

What does he mean by that? Coffee is quite powerful but is

that also considered a kind of drug?

He could justify himself by his daily work, but not for a soul like her.

What excuse remained for him? How could he lie so well? Or disguise what was so evident both inside and out their bodies and minds? She finally let it out.

"What the heck, I am supposed to tell the truth, am I not?" She sighed. So here it goes the truth:

"I am deeply in love with you, since the first time I laid my eyes over your, and I lost myself into that mysterious labyrinth from the deep blue of your sight."

She said that inside her head.

"I do not know anything about the case."

She sighed again.

"Please, please, release me. I have nothing to do with all of that crap. Like I told you before, I said everything I knew, and I even wrote it down on that notepad that your assistant just treated like a nasty scrap. Here is my confession and yet you don't seem to understand or to buy that. But I am as innocent as a lamb, and I could not possibly be related with that crime. Besides, I never touch any drug in my entire life. How am I supposed to know who were the drug dealers in that party?"

"But that Russian girl to whom you related in that party… the one who was accompanying you."

"What about her?"

"Did you know that she is involved with the organized crime and deaths, and with the drug dealers, including the recently case of the Brazilian guy who was at a party in Cancun and got involved with her and was just killed in Playa del Carmen in Mexico? And did you know that her boyfriend is the chief of them all, from the Russian mafia?"

She quivered.

No, she didn't know about nothing at all. If she knew who the girl was she would rather find a better company.

"Her name is Ekaterina Valierva."

"The blond girl with the snake tattoo in her neck? No, I didn't know about her personal life. I just knew that she was from Russia by her strong accent." That was all that she declared.

"You are in trouble, missy!" said another police officer who had just entered the room.

"I won´t say another word, I need my lawyer... let me call Art!"

The detective complained to the other officers that he could get a room for himself instead of exposing the lady to the crowd. In a fossil fashion, the competent officers who were squeezing each other through their elbows left the room as they spilled out the coffee from their cups over their uniforms.

His masculine facet leaded her to the individual room. It was so small that it only fit two people who could hardly place two chairs in each side of the table.

....

The woman went on to the toilet. Another blond with sunglasses was going inside the same changing room when they grabbed her arm. She looked at a man who was passing by.

"Call the police!"

"Misses Murphy? Stop there, ma'am!"

The receptionist still held her hands pressing them against her back.

"Call the police!!" He shouted out loud.

"Why are you doing this?" she said.

"I saw when you came with the other two guys. You were with them, weren't you?"

"No way! Let me go!" she screamed, desperately.

It was nine twenty and Misses Murphy was still on the toilet when the authorities arrived. The policeman left the Hotel with the blond and took the woman to the police station.

She tempted to look inside his files. And yet there was this wonderful feeling of an unrevealed sensuality that he captured from the young lady. She awaited him, impatiently. He let her go with no charges.

As she crossed to the other alley two men trapped her. She got rid of their hands and escaped off the streets. One man found her inside an alley. He tried to capture her, as he menaced to cut her throat.

During the struggle he cut the skin on the back of her wrist. She took his knife and pointed to his chest.

She inserted it deep. The man shouted in pain as she ran. But the other two men saw when she tried to get into a telephone cabinet, and they caught her.

They looked inside her eyes and saw that she was not the blond who they were looking for. The woman managed to escape once again.

"Now, we have to find our blond."

They returned to the hotel with the other blond. Misses Murphy opened the toilet's door: It was nine thirty-five. The other woman saw when the two men grabbed the blonde's arm and covered her head with a dark bag.

They left in a car with the billionaire's wife. The blond called a cab and followed them. They took the frightened woman inside an old building and wrapped her up with a strong metal.

The other blond girl was following them once again. But they didn't know it yet. How many blond girls could make a bond bold movie anyway??

One of the men, a six feet tall, dark haired and slim, lighted up a cigarette. The other guy was a short blond and had freckles all over his face.

"Now we have to ask for a ransom..." said the short guy.

"No, let's shut this woman out for good!" responded the tall man, with an incisive voice and penetrating dark eyes.

"But if you had promised we wouldn't touch her..."

"Shut up!" said the tall guy. He looked at his watch: it was nine forty-five.

"We don't have much time now. Let's go."

They left the building and went to a telephone booth.

The blond who had just followed the kidnappers from the hotel to the old neighborhood was waiting outside the building.

They didn't see her when they crossed the street to go to another telephone cabin. She followed them and tried to overhear their conversation.

"You call him!" said the tall man.

"No, you call him!!" answered the short blond guy, with his hand shaking while holding the telephone set.

"You chicken!" shouted the dark man. "You are incapable of making one stupid phone call!!"

The blond girl got even closer to the two men. She could hear what the tall man was saying over the phone...

"Yes, that's right! You heard me well: we've got her!" The tall man sounded even more enervated, "yeah, yeah, you hear it well: We got Misses Murphy... What? Yes, I said, Murphy, Misses Murphy!! Oh you mean morphine?"

The blonde was frozen in the chair, pale like a ghost and completely petrified.

"Now give us the money or else..." She ran to where they left the other woman.

When she arrived to the old building she heard a muffled scream. She knew the direction where the sound was coming from and she headed herself to the exact place where the woman was.

The woman had her head still covered with the black bag.

The blond saw a knife underneath the table. She also saw a revolver over the counter table. She then took the knife they left under the table. She partially uncovered the victim's neck, pinched the victim twice with her fake nail in her index finger.

A stream of blood ran from the holes down her neck making two vivid red lines from the two puncture points. The blond let the woman breath taking down the tape from her chin and cut the adhesive that they had put in the billionaire wife's mouth. She kissed her lips. The blond looked even more terrified.

"Good-bye, dear lover of mine! I can't stand seeing you married with this man." And she cut her throat. The tall man witnessed the whole scene.

"What the heck is going on?" He grasped.

"Thank God she was no billionaire's wife!" The other kidnapper shouted.

"So she's still on the loose!" The blond with a strong Russian accent said, looking vainly to her pointed nails. "What are you waiting for? Go find her!" she finally ordered.

She was too young to become a widow, and she didn't even get married. But her heart, well, that is another story, because she lived in parallel to another life, like a mirror: the life that she lived in Brazil.

Like magnetic poles those two lives would never get across but repulse, as two equal forces would only repel each other. That was most precisely to occur, unless the force between two parallel wires carrying currents is in the same direction which is always attractive. And this is repulsive only if they go in opposite directions. Like in a looping that her life had since been, it was up to her to make better choices.

Art comes to her house at ten. She doesn't answer his calls since the day before. He wants to see what is going on with the strange string of events. He arrives at Trenton Avenue. He parks the car near the corner.

He runs inside the building and he knocks at the door.

"Christie, it is me... Are you there?"

"Chris, are you..."

He hears a rumble. The floor shakes. He opens the door carefully. He also has her keys that she left with him.

"Use it just in case." He remembers her saying that.

Christie has her arms and legs spread all over the floor. He covers her body. Her whole body shivers.

"What did you do, Chris?" he started to cry. "I love you!"

But it is already too late. He takes his black coat and covers her body.

He takes her to the hospital. She is in a coma for about a week and half. They diagnosed her with inhaled anthrax. It was almost impossible to cure her then, for most of the cases of inhaled anthrax people fatally died.

He stays at the hospital holding her hand.

"Don't give up, baby!" He tells her.

And he kept talking to her while she is still, on her deep state of sleepiness.

And he always assured his love for her. Though he never was the kind of man to show his affections to the public eye, when they were in private he really got ignited with a flame so vast and strong that would keep her burning and eagerly asking for more and in burst of desires.

"I love you, girl, please, don't give up on me now."

They gave her antibiotics and other treatments. The doctors said that it was only a matter of time now. She was hardly breathing, and the bacteria had already attacked her blood stream.

The FBI was there as well. Gail Simon, who didn't know Art, introduced herself as a very close friend of Chris.

She said that she was very sorry that the place that she went to it was that ritualistic "party" in the Halloween but as a false flag it was already planned as an ideal spot for the terrorists to attack next.

They killed many people, making them believe that the white powder was cocaine, though it was actually the lethal biological weapon.

And that they then knew about her innocence, when she went to the place with her boyfriend, so distract, thinking it would be only a Halloween party. She wouldn't be sent to jail. She actually helped the police to solve the case. She was considered a heroin (and no pun intended) in the whole case.

And the heroin inside her bag was actually a pretension that they gave to her (that they were the ones who put that on her bag. They didn't say that, but it was quite obvious, anyway!) So that she would agree to cooperate with the investigators.

Art was puzzled. So she thought she was going to imprisonment. She who loved so much her own freedom? Freedom…

When was she free if she was surrounded by a fake security? So that's why she was acting so strangely lately.

"I didn't know she was that involved in this case!" He was troubled, but somehow he could articulate some words from what was really happening and matched some pieces up.

"But how come the terrorists invaded the party, if there was only so much security involved on that night? The parents were accompanying their own teenage daughters and sons, or at least one adult would accompany the children in their "treat or trick" leisure…"

It was too hard to conceive such a surrealistic effect that the whole scenario was composing over his head.

"…And any odd behavior would be considered as an attack?"

"I'm sorry, Art, that her boyfriend was a drug dealer. He didn't know about the ritual. That was all a "make believe". They were all playing of being in a kind of black magic stuff. The point is that the terrorists were disguised: in that party they allowed the masks, because it was supposed to imitate a tribal ritual. They would never think that they were actually inviting murderers to that party. But that is exactly what they were doing as they let people come so freely without any inspections on that party. They made innocent people be exposed by the white powder."

And the detective kept going on his evaluation of the situation:

"Many of them have now the symptoms of the flu, at least that is what they believe it is, and we cannot find the track of where those people are because they were afraid that the police would get them in prison, since the death of that young lady. That girl had such an enormous amount of anthrax in her lungs and stomach that she died right there."

Art was astonished. So many people didn't know that they had anthrax. They go to a party to have fun and they ended up being killed.

"Well, some of them had injuries in their skin. The skin cases are easily to be detected and also cured. They rapidly treat them with the antibiotics and the person can get better in a week or two and so they keep living their lives as if nothing had happened to them." He sighed.

"I am worried about the cases just like hers. She had made the test and it was negative for anthrax. Meanwhile, we are still investigating, because there are people out there that don't know yet, and, believe me, boy, they are hard to find."

"So, that means that even the terrorists were exposed?" Art is even more surprised.

"Why are you surprised? Isn't that obvious that the pattern of a terrorist is to kill himself, taking as many people as he can with him by doing so?"

Art couldn't believe his ears. There she was, the love of her life that he was so afraid to love for the lack of experience and for the fear of losing her forever, of ending up hurting her with his cold manners and his blunt way of saying things.

He had already done that to his mother. He always considered himself guilty for her death and there she was, the love of his life, practically dead in his arms.

"Go, take some rest." Gail smiled at him as she grabbed the patient's hand.

"You've been here for almost three days without really getting some sleep. Go home now. I will take care of her."

Art didn't move. He looked at Christie. She looked already dead.

Her beautiful shinny skin, with that tone of a healthy look that so many envy. She had such a gorgeous skin color and looked so tan that neither a month of the hottest days in a tropical paradise, nor a year on an artificial tan in a bed with the strongest rays would match her nuances.

And now it got the color of death. Her head looked so bloated like a soccer ball. It was pale, and gray and it lost texture. Her hands were as cold as the snow on the top of the Himalayan Mountains. But he kept holding her in his arms, embracing her, and kissing her lips, as he had never dared in his whole life.

"I am staying!"

Gail left the hospital room. It was a very moving scene: that of the boy in love with the girl in a coma.

Days passed and Christie didn't return from her coma. But Art didn't give up on her. He kept whispering in her ears. He sang her some of her favorites love songs. And one night he took her by his hands and he went to his knees.

He dropped his chin. She looked so divinely gorgeous, that goddess of a woman, that he had to look down not to let her seeing his crying. And he sang softly over her ears.

"Girl, I have a gift for you." He said. He did that in such an endearing way that she could not help and there she had some tears falling from her eyes. And yet she was paralyzed.

Christie didn't move, not even to slap off a fly that insisted on landing in her forehead away from her.

"I have a gift for you," insisted Art. "I paid you the College program fee. Now you can make the whole course without worrying about how you are going to pay it." And he started to cry.

"Why are you crying, my heart?

He looked up and he saw the face of his beloved smiling at him.

"I thought you were gone!"

"No, I am right here with you!"

Two months later they got engaged. She went to college and she finished graduation and soon she was able to work and she won her own fabric factory, and took her mother to be her partner. In fact her mother always thought Art as someone very similar to a character from the many books that she had already read.

He did resemble Frederick Henry in Hemingway´s novel *A Farewell to Arms*. After all, he also had a near death experience when he thought Christie would be taken from his life… and forever he did grow from it.

Five years after that miracle happened, Art asked Christie to marry him, and they had the most beautiful wedding in the city where they both were born.

In the middle of the ceremony Art asked Christie if she felt safe enough to allow him to take her to a dream that would last forever… a romance that would endure for the rest of their lives together.

"Would you hold your hands over my neck?" He said softly, while he carried her upstairs towards the alley. She laced her hands around his neck and touched his mouth very carefully with her left cheek. She could feel the warmth of his love embracing them both as if a veil that protected them from any harm could be seen from the invisible.

A pale violet light surrounded the couple. She looked at him, and he smiled at her. She instinctively searched for his lips, like a bird searching for water, and then they kissed each other avidly.

"I now pronounce you husband and wife. You may kiss the bride…" The priest's face turned into a red tomato just after hearing their vows for they had already made their statement in a physical demonstration. He finally gave them his blessings.

"Oh, you just did it, didn´t you!" The priest giggled as he looked at the audience, stupefied by what seemed to be way too obvious around lovers. "And they did it without my consent...by hook or by crook!

9

ALL SO FREAKING FISHY!

"I would like to take the great DiMaggio fishing", said the old man. "They say his father was a fisherman. Maybe he was as poor as we are and would understand." Hemingway in what would become his last novel *The Old Man and the Sea's* had analyzed his own situation in the end of his life. Pins and spins, hooks and tools, and other bait needles and needless to mention but this, that the old man was indeed Hemingway´s persona. And based upon this novel, Joe DiMaggio was a hero for him, representing a somewhat totem for the old man. His father was a fisherman and he came from a poor family. And at the time the book was written, DiMaggio had gone through unbearable pain as he had suffered from a bone spur. And he made a triumphal come back when he proved to be unbeatable. I sympathize with him for I too suffer from the same problem, and I keep dancing despite it all, being an athlete that´s the nature of the beast.

And just like Marilyn Monroe (and Misses Murphy) near the end, been completely hooked up, plugged in by the authorities to check on each and every act and step she took.

They were also addicted to prescription drugs that would then make them been taken by the hands of "specialists" and treated as a mental case.

So did Hemingway, who also had to go through a series of electroshock when he was in Clinica Mayo in Florida. He was being watched closely by the FBI, following his many staying at the Cuban Island. And, starting in the year 1942, he indeed did work for the Bureau on behalf of the American Embassy in Havana.

The writer had even declined an offer from Hollywood to write a script for a *March of Time* report about an American Volunteer group of fighter flying pilots in Burma and trained in China during the Second Sino-Japanese War. This would be a very revealing report when China fought Japan with the economic help of Germany, the Soviet Union and the United States. That before the fast and furious Fuhrer Adolph Hitler took the other way around and decided to go against the Soviet Union by evoking an alliance with Japan. So in 1940 the US was the main diplomatic and financial supporter of China.

And Hemingway preferred to dismiss all this great material for the script because he considered his working for the Bureau much more approachable and much more important. The Bureau thought that with his knowledge he could be of great help and be able to work for them. With a wide reputation as a fisherman he had a great acquaintance of the coastal lines of Cuba.

But Hemingway, with his free soul and wild nature, didn't think much before his attitude and he had already severely criticized the FBI by their acts early in 1940 by the arrests in Detroit concerning the recruitment in the Spanish Republican forces. And he had already stirred the pride of a member of the US Embassy when also back in 1940 he went against all protocols by presenting this particular person as Nazi and who preferred to be addressed as consul than a member of the Gestapo.

Hemingway apparently didn't recall any of those incidents and considered the Gestapo introduction as a prank; it seems that it's just like telling about the truth in a joking manner, it's more like a gag reflex! One may only convey that a man so literate would be more deliberate and choose wisely his own words.

He did indeed mean that. I mean, really!

Because the whole thing seemed too obscure to take it lightly, he had to use it as a joke.

Those links with the authority's policy and his working as an informant when he had been accused of being a Communist (which he had denied several times yet) couldn't go so far though. There in the FBI files there is an instance in a report made on December 19, 1942 where they were finally convinced that Hemingway had no particular love for the Bureau and could no doubt corroborate upon a campaign of vilification.

And his many activities were all a concern for those involved and they would become an embarrassment for them "unless something is done to put a stop to them", to quote the very same words from the FBI files.

"Has he been working as an undercover double agent?" They inquired.

By then Hemingway was already paranoid with his many "followers" (and not in the good sense as we may have today over the net). He was big fish for them to hook. A journalist and a great novelist who had such power over his hands and pen... So they shut him up, not directly, of course, but in a novelistic way.

Yes, his committing suicide was a fact, and affected all of us his fans and admirers. But he was drawn to do that so much earlier; after they have made his life miserable and so impossible to live, and after that they had already burned all his ingenious neural system.

And in the same sinister way as Marilyn Monroe, after he was not needed and became of no value for them, and worse than that, when he had pretty much turned out to be rather disruptive and actually a burden for them to take, that was when they had decided to terminate him.

And it was spatially and especially when Marilyn decided to open up her mouth to tell the world about the atrocities going on in Cuba and more specifically in the Bay of Pigs, after her involvement with the President and his top secrets that the CIA decided to shut her up for good.

Well, that it´s already written, and by the amount of people who already bought the book released last year (2014) and mostly by the reviewers, finally it was no big secret of who had killed MM.

And although I had written my book before "The Murder of Marilyn Monroe", they used the same title with the word "Murder", exactly the way I did two years before they had released it. And I had the means to prove it, although I kept the "Mysterious" word, for I guarantee you that it continues to be a great mystery, even for MM to know who exactly did plan the whole set up.

I guess someone wanted to take the glory upon his hands, to show to the world as a journalist and reporter that he knew what everybody already knew even in an indirect way. I was afraid to reveal all that, but then someone who is a "complete specialist" on Marilyn Monroe´s affair decided to release the book before I did, and had the "delicacy" to stamp a "CASE CLOSED" over her forehead in a picture taken of her from what would be her last film right there in the cover of his book. And it was not her best shot anyway. After all she was a "simple, warm bighearted (and heated) girl, that everyone took advantage of" (to quote her forever love, DiMaggio), and she is being taken for granted still, even today. And at least I´m not enlisted on that.

Let me tell you, Marilyn was not the least happy about the situation, in no way satisfied by being portrayed the way that she was in that book (and in so many others) with that evidence, and case proven by a man who did so little to care about her intimate life and search deep into her soul. She wants to tell more. So much so that it took her more three years to convince this writer here to finally put this book of mine out there. I guess I´m as stubborn as she was. (And there I hear her tittering, and it feels so right here and so close to my ear that her childish giggle tickles me and makes me laugh inside as well.) We´ve got so much in common… Maybe that´s why she felt inclined to come to me, and felt comfortable enough to share her feelings with me, and that I would feel entitled to do so.

There is so much in her soul, so much brightness that is so easy to be blind by her voluptuousness. And I keep it clean.

Ah, talking about beauties... When I was just starting my long-lasting career as a model a photographer told me I resembled both sisters Hemingway, but more the oldest one, who I presume now is Margaux. At that time I didn't even know who she was or heard about her. And exactly ten years later, actually the day that they found her dead, another make-up artist said I looked like her, "in her younger years", he said, while he managed to leave my hair with a wild aspect. And while feeling so close to her I could not leave Margaux Hemingway out of the picture. Her middle sister, Mariel, recently declared that her own father sexually abused Margaux several times when she was a child and shared the same room as her sister. And he did that not only to her but also inflicted this unbearable pain and left a scar forever on her older sister Joan too who has been in and out of mental institution since her sweet sixteen. No wonder Margaux was so disturbed. So beautiful and yet so tormented, so much so that she committed suicide when she was 41. In the end of her life, she was broken, leaving in a tiny apartment that the landlord insisted to her that she should get out and that so she did leave for he didn't like her "bad" vibes. She was hearing voices and she had a premonition that she was surely approaching her death and soon after that it came for her the end of the line.

It was intentional. But she didn't deserve to die, not like that and much less under the circumstances or in that day. Yet that's how her grandfather died and his father too, with a gun that Ernest earned from his suicidal father and requested to keep, although he would choose another gun to kill himself. And so did his brother who had Diabetes and as soon as he found out that he had to amputate both legs he shot himself to death. Surely enough in that family there should be forbidden the purchasing of guns.

Actually all guns should be banned forever from the face of the Earth. But there they would find so many other ways to choose to take their own lives, even if in a slower pace... like drinking heavily, for instance, only that this is a painful type of suicidal mode, can also take the liver to malfunction until it can no longer work properly.

Of course, mental health and depression is in the calendar. The Hemingway's were like the Kennedy's. They were all American families, always in the spotlight living fancy lives for public view and scrutiny, filled with traditions and tragedies. To be vague and in vogue all the time would take a toll in their own lives.

One can even dare call it "a curse"! In the case of the Hemingway's there were so many cases running in the family that one can only wonder if it has something to do with Karma.

A Karmic sense that there is something running in the family which is quite not right and you have to struggle to battle this beast out of your system. Some people cope with it, some don't. The most gifted and creative and geniuses members of the family usually are also the ones who suffer the most. They are more disturbed and cannot actually live a "normal" life.

And so it was the case with Marilyn, Her mother also suffered from mental disease, and she had to be taken to a foster care for her mother was put in a mental institution. Adele Hugo, the youngest daughter of Mister Victor Hugo, the great French writer (and by the way my grandmother's cousin) was also put in a mental institution. Her uncle, brother of Monsieur Hugo, Eugene, had already been diagnosed with schizophrenia. And so did Camille Claudel, the great artist and sculptor and Rodin's pupil/lover who had several thoughts of suicide and lived in a sedated stance and attached to a bed for thirty years when she finally died as she was about to complete seventy-nine.

But there is an atmosphere of mystery and tragedy in the case of MM. Even though some tried to unveil the knot hovering over her murder, there are still some missing pieces... I guess it would take another lifetime to investigate it more deeply and finally find the real perpetrator.

"He was a traitor!"

Who said that?

"Yes, indeed, he was…"

It all worked like a smokescreen. First you shoot some random people than in the middle of the commotion you shoot your target, and you aim for it, and back on shooting other people who has nothing to do with the case, and there you have it. No one is certain of the real motives. It´s the same M.O. making it all appear as coincidental only that it´s made on purpose.

Only that when you watch it on movies and read on some mystery books you never think this would actually happen. And yet this happens just around the corner. It touches down a little too close to you. And it may sometimes even happen in your neighborhood.

"It´s like the Sniper case in Washington D.C. and what we are seeing here is a real life mystery."

"No kidding! One of the men who were killed by the sniper was my dentist´s friend. He was mowing the lawn doing a big favor to a friend during the weekend when he got shot. And after that there was the FBI agent who got shot as she was coming from the grocery to her car in the parking lot." She says, in a shot and almost without breathing. The heat penetrates her skin when the detective looks right to her perplexed eyes.

The vision of this beautiful lady alone in the room with a strong man would arouse the most flat of the human beings. He pulsates by his own instinct. He shakes her heart and she can hardly breathe.

"It is too hot in here, don't you think so?" she tells him.

The sound of a bell is heard from the streets.

"I am sorry! Would you like me to turn the air conditioning on?"

"YOU turn me on!" she thinks to herself.

"It is cool outside, but indeed very warm in here."

He smiles. Oh, no, stop smiling! Let's go back to work…

He turns his back and grabs a fan. He is going to be turned into an obsession in her own world, if he continues to let her

THE MYSTERIOUS MURDER OF MARILYN MONROE

deserve his seat as a stranger in the night that comes to rescue her. She looks at his jeans as he turns his back to her. She likes what she sees from behind.

What a nice pair of jeans! But she is here for a serious matter. He must save her from the arms of the evil, which is her boyfriend Dawson. But isn't he her stepbrother too?

He comes back. His hands and lips tremble. He cannot disguise the tension that he feels towards her. He looks at her chest. Her breasts are showing off for him, like saying, "Look, boy, here we are... come and catch us!"

Her nipples appear through the fine tissue. They dance and bounce from her shirt and right into his face, showing off the tan skin contrasted with the white cotton fabric. He stops his breath and waits for the worst. They bounced. Moving forward they almost like wave at him. Then they finally stop moving. She sits down for his relief.

"Oh, she just forgot to wear bras!" He thinks to himself.

"So, tell me, what do you know about that girl," he asks her, "since when do you knew her?"

"Not much... Like I told you that night!"

The plot gets bigger the harder they shake it.

"What about your boyfriend. Did you talk to him after that incident?"

"Oh, yeah. That is right! I talked to him. He doesn't know anything about the girl."

She gets up from the chair. And it seems like she had just seated in glue, so stinky and sticky it feels inside her underwear.

"Can I go now?" she says out loud and in a dry humor, and with the slightest idea where that sly personality was coming from. Since she stood there for hours with no clue whatsoever of what she was doing there it is definitely time to leave.

He touches her shoulder. He strikes it carefully, but insistently enough that his sweating starts to irritate her bare skin.

"Sit down, please." He tells her in an assertive, irresistible way. "Things are getting more complicated here. We are looking for a clue, which is kind of hard to find, since the girl died of an overdose…" He pauses for a while. It seems like he is about to cry when he looks up at her and continues with his monologue. She looked at his lips as he moves them slowly and in an irresistible sexy vibration, opening slightly too as he almost touches his upper lip and then refreshing it up with a sip from his tongue.

"…And she also had some injuries."

What injuries? She realizes that his mouth is surrounded with small sandy, granulated yellow particles like head ruffs... should she says dead rough?? And he tries to swallow it.

Oh, that's disgusting! And she who was about to search on the net for his name to find if he was a famous detective or something... Such a shame! Such a handsome man with saliva to die for... really, literally, to die for the smell and the grotesque form!

She has her mouth open. Not open voluntarily by that vision, but he opened her mouth to take some sample from her own saliva. After that quick check up she kept her mouth open.

And it was not because of what he had said to her, nor for what she saw in his dried lips. It is just that she didn't expect them to connect her in any way with that woman.

"…And the problem is now that you are involved into this case, since we found some traces of heroin in your purse."

"What?" She said looking for something inside her purse. She examined it upside down and inside and out, she was exasperated. She hesitated and then continued rambling…"Who put that on my purse? On my "Black-hole"…" That is how she called that big bag that she carried everywhere and she used to hold just to hide a small pepper spray bottle to provide her some security as walked on the streets. Being victimized was not her deal. "Who did that to me? Someone is playing dirty here. You did that, didn't you?"

"Calm down. Calm down. We are not saying that you are a criminal or something. We don't have any suspect yet. Besides your boyfriend, of course, who we know have a direct link to the crime… We are just trying to find some other connections."

"Look. You were very nice that night, but I am being threatened here now. I have no connections with that girl. Didn't you hear me? No connections. So, please, just let me get out of here."

"Wait a moment!" said another officer who entered abruptly in the room.

"Your life has been investigated and it looks like your boyfriend had a very disturbing childhood. Did you know that?"

She looks around and sees her reflection in the mirror. It was then that she noticed that the mirror was not really about her reflection, but there was someone behind the mirror. They were watching in her every move closely throughout a one-way glass.

"No, I didn't know that."

She was so surprised by the whole thing that she looked at both men in that interrogation chamber as if they were coming out of a surrealistic picture. She felt herself framed inside a piece of theater where she didn't rehearse and thus didn't know whose line was it, anyway. So they were all real actors.

"And they expected me to act like that too?" she thought. "Am I supposed to be the star from this play; or a mere display?" That is exactly how she was feeling…like a display…a doll in the hands of those playful actors…

"Yeah, yeah, sure you do. You must have known by now. This guy is screwed. He already had some records, being twice sentenced into prison."

"Oh, my goodness, Dawson had a dark side that I never knew and I never dreamed of knowing." There she sits like she carries a heavy load over her shoulder. She could never think that a man who seemed to be so in love with a woman could hide all that from her. "And why would he do that?"

"He was incarcerated before…for stealing. He is a burglar. Did you know that?"

"Oh, man!" she fought against what she was hearing. She feels a strange tingling sensation all over her head now. "That I didn't know. My God! Is he screwed or what? And am I screwed now?

"You better get your friend's address to us right away, or you are the one to be in trouble here as a retriever of proofs. Or you could also be considered an alibi for a crime."

A cold stream of odd sensation prevailed all over her spine. Now she was feeling cold. No more the warming passion that made her feel so secure at her hero's arms, but now she could feel the harsh cold wind coming from the fan.

But that is still not the final sentence. The sentence was to give her boyfriend to the hands of those policemen who seemed to care less about her feelings than for her boobs appearing inside her silky blouse, loosely bouncing freely, so much the opposite as she was feeling now. And there they seem to have an incisive glimpse aiming directly at her breasts so closely and not careful enough to take their eyes off, with much more eagerness than the whole story of a murder.

Long story short, they got her working with an undercover agent, which is fine for her. For not going to prison, she let them live her life for a while, and see how hard it is to be a young lady living by herself nowadays.

There are two agents taking care of her case: one is a middle aged woman who would help her find where the murder is. And there is another man, a fat guy, who prefers to be called just as Jay.

Gail Simon, that is her name, wants to play the role as the girlfriend who she does not see since her childhood in the suburbs of D.C. and that now appears in her life, tired of her suburban life looking for adventure.

She will have to make it all out. Now she does have a girlfriend who she doesn't see for years and she will have to introduce her to her boyfriend.

"Probably she will try to seduce him, they will both go to bed, and then they can all go to hell as well!"

Oh, man! That is getting really complicated.

"Oh, Dawson, you damned son of Dawn... only if you were not so handsome!"

....

A Ransom in a pretty awesome amount..

Ten minutes past ten pm. They were expecting the blond to get out of that toilet soon. Another blond woman with sunglasses went inside the same changing room. When she left they kidnapped her instead.

The kidnappers left the Hotel with the blond. She got rid of their hands and escaped off the streets. But the other man saw when she tried to get into a telephone cabinet, and they caught her back again.

"Now, we have to find our blond." The other blond managed to escape once again. They left in a car with who they thought was the billionaire's wife.

The blond called a cab and followed them. They took the frightened woman inside an old building and wrapped her up with a strong metallic rope.

"Now we call the billionaire demanding the ransom."

The blond came inside the building and inserted the same knife that they had left over the table deep into the chest of the billionaire's wife:

"You bitch! Take it! You took him from me, now I take you from him." She said with her strong Russian accent.

"Hey, wait!" said the kidnapper.

"Don't you tell me that she's no billionaire's wife!!

....

"The allegations against Dawson could charge him for at least fifty years in prison!" Gail told her.

She starts to cry. She never thought that such a thing could possibly happen in her life. A man who she dreamed of one day would ask her hand in matrimony is going to jail. And she is about to complete twenty next month. No, not twenty men in her life, you naughty! She was only nineteen…

"You know that I was planning to marry him?"

"Yes, you told me that," said Gail with a complacent eye, "like five times!" She dried her tears with a tissue that she had carried in her purse. "After all you grew up together, you said that he was twelve when you mother decided to adopt him…"

"He was like an angel to me, no one could ask for a better step brother… And I would step all over him and he would still do anything to see me happy. Anything and everything I would ask him to do, and he's just everything to me!"

"Who's your daddy?"

"What?" Christie asked.

"I mean, if you are that important for him, where is he now to help you out to clean up this mess?." said Gail, in a very honest tone. She had made her point.

"A series of allegations of black magic and sessions with fetishes are being investigated." Gail sighed and then she continued with her weird explanations. Who cares?

"I don't care what she thinks of that all. I just want to be left alone." Christie whispered. Inside her head it was another story.

157

A brainstorm was forming very quickly and Gail was really getting into her nerves now.

Alone!! Did you hear me?

"They video recorded the murder of innocent people, and the torturing to death of women ages between thirteen and thirty is also part of the investigation," Gail continued into her dissertation. "And I think your dear friend is very involved. It is kind of risky now. If I were you I would not go out with this guy ever again. And please do stay away from his companions. They might be very dangerous too. Your dear friend almost took you to your own death, remember!" No, she doesn't want to hear her anymore. And she won't even listen to her own thoughts...

"But he is my boyfriend, and I have feelings for him. Besides, his friends were always very nice to me. I may be upset with the way things happened, but I've been going out and I know his friends since I was five years old."

"You better be careful, girl. Tomorrow, you will call your friend."

Gail touched her with kindness. "But, by now do not get too close. Just mention about the friend who is visiting you, ok?"

The plot is ready. She might as well incarnate the scene and be part of the game or else she would suffer even more serious consequences. She might get fatally hurt otherwise. But how much more injured will she be than that? Her heart was bouncing back and forward, she could not even internalize her own feelings and she was expected to act and react naturally to everything that has been going on in her life lately. They also think that's just too much to grasp for her. But they trust her instincts.

She tried to disengage from the situation. But every move she makes seem pointless. She cannot get away from this anymore than she could get away from her own truth. She has to play her part. And she can hardly breathe. She looks at her leg: it has a little cut, but the scar will stay forever. It was a deep cut. But even more difficult to deal with that it would be the profound scar that started to appear on her consciousness. Little she would imagine then that the worst was yet to come.

Happily Ever After the Rescue

It was ten o'clock. They were expecting the blond to get out of that toilet soon. Another blond woman with sunglasses went inside the same changing room. They grabbed her arm, and they left the Hotel. She got rid of their hands and escaped off the streets. But they captured her and also the other girl.

Now they left in a car with both the blond and the billionaire's wife. They took the frightened women inside an old building and wrapped them up with a strong adhesive material.

"Now we call the billionaire demanding the ransom." They left the building. The blond took the knife which was hidden inside her sleeve, let it slip to her wrist and then grabbed it.

"It's all right, girl! I am a police officer, and I am going to take you out of here." She cut the wrapped material from the blonde's lips. It was then that she noticed there was a red tip of a fake nail inserted in her neck.

"It must have been from that Russian lady who insisted on offering me a drink and almost forced me to take it at that party, grabbing my neck and pulling me towards her glass."

"You are probably right. Don't you move, and let me take this off of you," said the policewoman, carefully taken that piece of nail from inside her skin. She took a closer look and added, "...or they became a bit more sophisticated after those failed kidnapping three times in a row and decided to track you down instead by using a cheap chip with a GPS." She took it even closer and the material shined against her eyes. "My team and I will later on analyze it in the lab .I'm assuming that it was the only way that they got to make you be recognized among the crowd!"

The billionaire's wife couldn't contain herself and kissed the police officer passionately. She asked the billionaire for a divorce for she had just decided to marry the policewoman. She called her daughter eagerly to tell her the big news.

"Christina, you are invited to my marriage." Her mother said.

On the other side of the line there was a devouring silence. It was terrible enough to know that she could not make anyone fall in love with her.

But then to finally live to hear that her own mother was about to getting married... and again! Christina looked at her watch for the last time as she had just died inside: it was ten minutes after ten. Well, at least that was what she thought then. It would take more five years until she could finally marry her soul mate, her heart, dear Art.

10

IN THE NEW YORK MINUTE

When I lived in Los Angeles, California, the first thing I noticed every morning from my windowpane it was that polluted air that seemed to stick forever over the hills like a printed Black-and-White picture near the busy airport. And although I had my HQ (as in the Heart Quarter) in Santa Monica, and feeling that ocean breeze and fresh wind in the Pier was already delightful, not even cruising on the colorful Boulevard or through the exhilarating Organic Farm Market, or in between boats in Marina Del Rey would uplift all spirits. Nevertheless, I care not (and I dare not) to miss at all the smog or the smell of smoke and diesel around the area. But, at that time, I was still drifted upon the Gardenia fragrance from my prior trip to Hawaii. I just missed so much my favorite flavor that nothing could beat that perfume, except the coffee and sugarcane tastes from the harbor in my sweet birthplace in Santos, Brazil.

Then I got married and moved to the suburbs in Washington. Again I had to get used to a different smell, of a multicultural facet and fragrance that still today I miss after living there for three and a half years and leaving then for more than ten years already. How not to if in the spring there is always that breathtaking beauty of the cherry blossoming in the front and the backyard of my former condo. During the fall, the delicate wind brings about the scent of wet and organic sensation through a mixed essence of the perspiration of the earth spread through a carpet of the red and orange leaves on the ground. And the winter seemed to stick out the best odor from the pine trees contrasting with the white snow in the forest that pictured my window, where sometimes I could see a red fox, or a couple of deer, searching for some food. And even the stink from the ice covered with salt touched our nostrils with candor. All tastes offer a bouquet of choices and memories recollecting a sense of enlightenment of just being alive. But there are some smells that stay in your heart forever and yet you better off try not to pull that memory too often.

A week before September Eleven a bird crashed against the sash. Two feathers remained in that same pane of glass that had witnessed so many changing of seasons, and yet had displayed some ethereal scenery, all of which already inspired me to write three novels. I thought the scene was so spooky that I cried my lungs out. Just after that I went to Canada with my husband by car. We passed through New York three days before the 9/11. He wanted to stop there. I didn't, and for my relief he complied.

"I see a dark cloud over this city. I don't know but I don't like being here. Let's get the heck out of here. And let´s do it quickly!" I didn't have a vision, although that eerie sensation was persistent. I actually saw a black cloud exactly over the towers. Then in the morning of that tragic day we were in Canada. We turned the TV on. We saw there was a strike on the frontier. And we were worried about not being able to go back home.

"Now we cannot go back to the States." I said angrily.

All of a sudden they stopped showing the strike and what
appeared to be a fire on a building came on the TV screen.
We could not quite get what was going on. And then when we
saw the other plane crashing the other tower we were shocked
and numb. I looked at that scene again and again in disbelief.
After a few seconds, and only then that I knew that America was
under attack and I went down on my knees and I started to pray.
That seemed the only reasonable thing to do by then.

"Please, God, there let not be a war, please, I'm begging you!"
I looked at that beauty in front of me. I had a panoramic view of
the lake and tower in Quebec. I saw people walking down the
streets as if nothing happened. It was a beautiful day, the sun
was shining and I could see all that from the hotel room through
the window and the floor where I was still kneeling down started
to shake. It was me in shock, choking with my desperation.
Outside everything looked so perfect, like a Renascence
painting, and I was sobbing, shaking in the same place like the
wings of a humming bird in flight, crying my eyes out and with
the world around me still. "Now we cannot go back to the
States!" I finally said, desperately.

Time is an illusion. Just in a few seconds I had passed from a
state of powerless but arrogance to a state of completely stupor
and humility. What five seconds can do to your life! Five days
later, on a sunny Sunday morning, we were back to New York
City. The smoke was still out there after almost a week. And I
could feel that intoxicating stench of burning, of ashes, of death,
so acrid that it reminded me of the strong radioactive emission
that I sensed on a sole piece of atomic debris from Hiroshima,
lost in the middle of the hall in the United Nation Building.

Like Adam and Eve, we were also exiled, away from the
Paradise. We had to go away from the place that we always
knew as safe and cozy. And so we left. The place where we got

used to call home, so far away from our own hearts now, since hell touched base.

She went to the party close to the Marriott Hotel, in the subway, near the escalator from the Metro, underground Juniper Street in Philadelphia. Someone held her a paper where it described the way Pennsylvania was settled.

Sylvan means "jungle" and Penn is the founder of the Quakers and he got this entire "jungle" as a payment from a debt of King Henry (or Charles III, but I pretty much think the latter inherited this debt from him).

Then he founded Philadelphia, which means the city (Delphos) of the brotherly Love (Philos). It is quite interesting to know that the Quakers were protecting the natives and that they all thought that everyone, regardless of sex, ethnic origins, color or culture, all people have the right to freedom for everyone of us have this light from God burning deep inside.

But, anyways, she just felt as if she was not invited here, since she was not really invited. They look at her as if she were a stranger. She actually WAS a stranger. She was an alien, all right. There she was something she always felt like anyway, an alien living in the USA.

The images of witchcraft, demoniac calls, magic, and even Satanism felt so horrendous, yet so close to our times. The last movies directed to children have all been about supernatural powers, but the kind of power that will only destroy:

Where is the moral in *Maleficent* (and Angelina Jolie, who had the main role in that movie didn't allow her own children to watch it, God knows why!), *Harry Potter* (magic), *The Twilight Series*, about witches, vampires and werewolves that showed only shape-shifting and other horrendous images to children when what they most need is a model to follow?

Where is the need to show so much violence on TV and on games made for children to play? It's not that we don't have violence in this world. *"Au contraire, ma soeur et mon frère"*.

You just need to tune into a channel that just shows it indefinitely.

But how about showing some grace, some peaceful plots, some stories about redemption, are they so hard to find? Not at all. They need as much energy as we spend producing some horrible content. Are the humanity so thirsty for blood? I remember being a child and watching movies on TV that showed vampires and other terrifying scenes.

How much I feared them, and just like Margaux (Hemingway) I felt troubled and was eager to get the hell out of the places and bad influences that had been bothering me. So back on talking about my "look-a-like" and, eerily enough, a month after I left Santa Monica, and a day before it completed thirty-five years of his grandfather Ernest Hemingway's suicide that's when and where she died. In her final years she looked terrible in a B-movie about some weird stuff. Yet she was trying to find peace by turning to more spiritual doctrines.

Only she went through some wrong hands. And in some way she was longing to find a way out of this ordinary world, to have a deeper experience, which would allow her to change life from upside down to something bigger, and more connected to the divine power.

Humanity always had this fascination with the realms of the unknown and the supernatural. But only if we knew that we've got that power inside ourselves. Only we have been too lazy to step forward and tune it in. So we just let the outside control us and its manipulative way had been destroying our natural ability in the most dreadful form. Expect more movies about the war as we get closer and closer to a final countdown. Is that some kind of prophecy? No, it's just the way things are turning, unless...

"Unless, what?"

"Unless we change our ways..." She said, her eyes turning inward now.

THE MYSTERIOUS MURDER OF MARILYN MONROE

A black cat passed through her way. The cat looked at her and she could sense an ironic atmosphere in the air. It was October, 31 of 2001.The first Halloween that she was about to spend away from home. It was the first one from the new Century and the first blue moon that she had ever experienced in America.

The only thing that she didn't know yet (and that she had to learn later anyway) it was that a wish always comes true. But, sometimes, it is simply not exactly as we planned that to be.

Her own life was about to change. Right! But from upside down to an everlasting snowball, increasing the crisis in size and diminishing in hopes of getting better. Like a huge roller coaster transforming it into a monster that she wouldn't happen to manage, unless she could see the vision of a giant red signal. And it was not the red light watching her constantly in the obelisk, that blinking menacing source in that tower, while she was flying away from D.C. That force was nothing comparing to what she had to face yet.

And she would only be able to stop it if she could just stop it right when she noticed the first signals of danger... Because the solutions of her problems were also available to her and that she knew she could reach it at the tips of her fingers.

If only she could see that on time…

He seated at the Central Park on a bench near the lake.
He was certain of already making too many mistakes.
Yet he could not help but think he had failed somehow.
She was gone for over ten years, gone without a bow.

Those were the golden days when they used to fake
with each other in happiness, strolling along that lake,
That brought too many remembrances and sorrows.
For them there will not be no longer a tomorrow.

She had almost drowned, not quite on that lake,
In a sea of passion because her life was at stake.

168

But all that he found was his pride to swallow.
So he buried her into a deep and dark hollow.

He tried to keep her on track and he had failed.
He knew deep inside their entire life yielded.

He knew that she suffered from a mental inability
It was not even a matter of sense, but sensibility:
She fell right at the beginning of their marriage.
The pain she endured counted as a lot of mileage.

After all the advices that he received from their friends,
he denied the existence of any turbulence and trends.
He insisted on trying to keep things smooth
But the boat was about to sink in sooth.

He should have seen that coming, but yet...
He was too dull and he couldn't see it wet
His mind got lost in a dizzy kaleidoscopic din.
It passed like a ball running directly to the pins.

Their fifth anniversary they would celebrate.
He left her a note, before it was too late.
Although he knew she would not be that far.
It was the last time he would let the door ajar.

She was already gone, so...
He released her from his soul
and stopped feeling sorry for him.
There was nothing else for them to deem.

He decided to live his own life once again.
As if a tender kiss blessed a child right then,
A cold breeze blew right through his face.
Ans he felt the warm and delicate embrace.

He smiled as he received the lace,
Coming by the sweet sunshine rays.
Calling his name the rain softly fell
In each drop there he heard the bell.

He then felt the ethereal sunshine over his left ear.
And he heard her whispering, "Good-bye to you, dear!"
He then breathed in deeply and felt such a bliss
that now he knew she found a place called "Peace".

The September, Eleven (or the new Pearl Harbor) that changed the world forever served as a smoke screen to distract people with Terrorism and fear of more attacks.

That was planned much earlier and just before the Gulf War, which already had people in London crazy about a terrorist attack, I was there in the subway and there were signal everywhere telling us to watch our backs and any bags left unattended. Scary as hell, heels over heads about the news of hostages taken by terrorists in a kidnapping of commercial airplanes. But that seemed so distant from America. So there should have a bigger plan to make people really scared to death and let their surveillance touch their lives and control their steps completely.

And the fact that the attacks on the Twin Towers and on the Pentagon were just means to an end, a way of destroying real evidence, with files and records about the Kennedy's assassination, and also of the murder of Marilyn Monroe by the CIA, along with proofs of the existence of a powerful weapon, the mind control program, and of an alien intelligence behind it all.

There is no doubt the collective consciousness is most infatuated with many Conspiracy Theories. And a note from Marilyn herself, just after she died, by the hands of a Medium (the same one that is now writing these words) only shows that nothing can be kept in the dark, and some way, somehow the Divine Justice shall prevail and the Truth will always comes to light.

"I didn't kill myself, no... If I was going to remarry Joe (DiMaggio)☐within a week of that horrible death, how that could possibly come out in my head... there was no suicidal thoughts by then. Gosh! It just makes me so sad that people would still think and or want to believe what the official press says. That's so depressing. It makes me sick to my bone that they do believe them. Of course I tried to kill myself or at least thought of doing so (and who didn't) more than once, twice, thrice, perhaps. But I didn't kill myself, I swear. I don't want to reveal who did it, but I guess people pretty much know by now. At least my most devoting and adoring fans and genuine admirers must know. And no, I wasn't afraid of getting gold. I mean old! I was just thinking how beautiful it would be to have kids or in the last possibility I would adopt a kid and then we would get older and I would live to see my grandchildren, and I would teach them how to dance, how to sing, how to act. Of course they would follow my steps and even join in a new Rat Rack.... (Giggles) I crack... hahahaha! Pack. That's what I said. The Rat Pack which was one helping the other, with true devotion, like the guys did for me. I cannot say that I'm happy about what happened, the way that it happened, the revenge and all. But I have to confess that I was too naïve and even vanity took over me when I decided to reveal everything all due to my own ego, and because of a broken heart, I would tell everyone our own president talked to the little green men. And I would tell all that of what he told me in confidence." And what he told her in the end were basically truths that they kept secret for way too long. President Kennedy was the last one of the American presidents who knew about that all.

- A statue has been removed from a spacecraft. Such object has supernatural powers with cosmic ritualistic hieroglyphic signs that once serving as a form of incantation may cause imbalance between the two opposite poles and which forces may bring creation or destruction.

- The secret weapon that the CIA has been searching for and that have been taken from the spaceship that it is now in the hands of a secret sect.

- The CIA believes those who got this machine want to use it as a weapon to restore what they call 'The New World Order.'

- President Kennedy knew about the whole ordeal and actually was the last of the American Presidents to know about this weapon and had direct contact with the Extra-terrestrial visitations.

That same statue which was used by the Czechoslovakian man killed only two months before her murder, that alien figure with the magical hieroglyphic was to be exploited to gain victory against the enemies. That's how Pele got injured during the second game at the World Cup in '62. And just after that he had his kidney removed. It was after a broken rib, and he was advised to take off the organ that was malfunctioning and ruining his health. And he already lost before he could even win, it was a secret that he kept well guarded until a few weeks ago when he had to go through a kidney treatment. But as the same talisman that plays its own rules, of cause and effect, any given subject who uses it in the wrong way would suffer serious consequences. Thus, just after that second act, in the game played in that violent World Cup in Chile, that the man got killed and the magical talisman has been missing ever since.

If they could do this to the king Pele, what could they do with the Mortal Goddess Marilyn Monroe, who had the most valuable talisman of all, her huge heart of gold and such a generous soul?

CPSIA information can be obtained
at www.ICGtesting.com
Printed in the USA
BVOW04s1848281116

469110BV00001B/82/P

9 781329 051195